LEAD
WITH
SUCCESS

*Powerful Stories From Women
That Will Help You Lead With Success*

Raquel Cordova | Patty Dominguez | Anna Martinez
Mia Perez | Andrea Ocampo | Sandylu Guerrero
Pamela Valenciano | Teresa Razo

Disclaimer: Thank you for buying and reading this book. The authors wanted to share their experience and knowledge with you that could potentially improve the quality of your life and the lives of others. Spanish is the native tongue for most of the authors and this is their first of many books. Despite their noble intentions, this book will have mistakes like any other book. If you find any mistakes, PLEASE tell us by sending the error and page you found it on to our email LeadWithSuccessBook@gmail.com. We thank you and appreciate your feedback. We would like to wish only the best for you and your families.

Table of Contents

Foreword

Patty Arvielo, President & Co-founder,
New American Funding

When I was approached if I would consider writing a forward for *Lead with Success*, I felt honored, surprised, and even a little nervous. After all, this work is a collection of exceptional success stories told by extraordinary women.

Truth is, I never pass up an opportunity to share about female empowerment. It's an incredible feeling knowing I may be a woman who is looked up to, the way I have looked up to other women along my journey. I am a strong believer that as women, we should come together and support each other, very much like Sheryl Sandberg says, "Lean In". It is my hope that by sharing our failures and our successes, and the thoughts and emotions that go along with them, these stories will resonate with other women.

If you've picked up this book looking for inspiration, encouragement, or a source of empowerment, you won't be disappointed. Sometimes just a few simple words will make something click, and spark that underlining energy propelling you to go out and do more.

Life has presented many of us with challenges that at the moment seemed to be impossible to overcome. However, it is our innate passion to keep moving forward that binds us together. At times we may experience self-doubt, worry, or loneliness, but we have found ways to push forward. From times of confusion to the moment you discover your angel mentor, this book speaks to struggles of self-worth and personal triumph.

Lead with Success is a compilation of amazing and inspiring stories with one common denominator, women filled with passion and courage that have overcome serious adversity. Impossible is simply not in our vocabulary! Read on, be inspired and remember no one will tap you on the shoulder and ask you to be successful. This drive is in all you!

Introduction

Lead With Success is a book written for the purpose to inspire others like yourself to persevere through your struggles and to keep fighting for towards your dreams. Our country is soon going to elect a new president and it seems like we are divided now more than ever before. Most people think that the decisions of the new President will improve or diminish their quality of life but in all reality this is normally not the case. The thousands of decisions we make on a daily basis will either move you towards or away from your life goals and ambitions. This book was written by 8 powerful Latina influencers who united together and are dedicated to improving the quality of life for our communities. It's time for American Latinas and Latinos to unite together along with other ethnicities to take a stand for a better tomorrow for our children. The world is hungry for leadership and we want to do our part with by sharing our stories in this book.

CHAPTER ONE

A Rebel With A Cause

My Journey To Chicago

I distinctly remember making the BOLD decision and saying to myself, *"This is where they might want me to be, but this is not where I want to be."* What I needed to do for myself was pretty evident, but we always want to doubt ourselves and question what we already know to be true for ourselves. It is a constant battle that may never end in the human mind. I am just bold enough to talk about it...

I was in a new city, Chicago, Illinois. A beautiful city it was. A grand city, with HUGE buildings, very rich in history, and very magical. I have always been a big city girl, with big city dreams. The bridges, the taxis, the streets, the hustle and bustle, the movement, the bums asking for money, women wearing business suits yet sporting tennis shoes and walking fast, making sure they get to the train so they can get home to their families. It was a different type of rush for me. I was not used to this kind of movement being a California girl. I am hyper, but this movement within the city excited me. To top it off, I was on my own.

Yes, a young 22-year-old girl living in Chicago with nothing but a roommate who was also a radio personality at the same station I worked for. I had this whole city to myself to explore, make new friends, finding new spots to shop and get my haircut. It was scary, yet I was ready to take on a new city with a whole new challenge, Spanish radio! The format was actually a Mexican regional format, which is not what I was used to. I grew up listening to hip-hop, R&B, Celia Cruz, Grupo Niche, La India & Tito Puente, so Mexican regional music was never really my cup of tea. I had to keep reminding myself it was a sacrifice and a learning experience and that every day had an intention, which was to make me a better radio personality. However, the loneliness was REAL.

I missed my family, my nephew, mom, dad, sister, brother; all that was familiar to me was temporarily gone. I was in such a state of discomfort, but the little voice inside me always told me I was on the right path. Even when things felt weird, scary, or new for me, I knew I had to go through it. A big part of my success I like to attribute it to be me being out of my comfort zone a lot.

Life has always had a way of putting me in uncomfortable situations so that I could grow, and with no surprise I always do. I figure out a way. I get shit done. Being out of your comfort zone makes you move. It is like imagining yourself walking on hot coals. You know it is entirely possible and that you might get burnt a little bit, but you will survive. That is how I felt about my whole Chicago experience. This was all part of the stretch.

I believe we are meant to be stretched in order to learn the lesson … but never break. Stretch not break, remember that. My Chicago experience for me was one of my big stretches. I clearly remember flying out of LAX (Los Angeles international airport) and seeing LA get smaller and smaller wondering when I would be back. It was a feeling that til this day I cannot describe.

I had no car when I first arrived in the windy city, so my only form of transportation was train. Eventually, when I did get my car, I will never forget when I tried to drive in the snow, I freaked out. It was early in the morning like 3:30 am; I was doing the morning show, so I was up before the roosters were.

In Chicago, when it snows, the snowmobiles are out clearing the streets of snow so that people may drive to get to where they need to go. I remember approaching a red light and as I tried to stop my care kept sliding. Thank God it was early in the morning, and there were hardly any cars out. So there I am, a girl that's new to the windy city, stuck in the middle of an intersection in SHOCK. My heart was pounding. If there would have been cars I probably would have crashed head on. I continued to drive so carefully, but I was nervous the entire way to the radio station. To top it all off, I get to downtown Chicago where the radio station was and park. That day I discovered that parking in downtown was like $35; yeah, that was the last day I ever drove to work.

I am a Cali girl that is used to jumping in a car and going to my destination. Chicago is much different. Most people in the city depend on the train to get to work. The radio station happens to be on Michigan Ave right in the heart of Chicago. I could literally see Michigan Lake from the building I worked in. I now had become one of those girls that depended on the train to get home and to sometimes get to work because my ride did not always necessarily wake up on time to pick me up. It was an entirely different life than I was used to living. I went from a small city, Palm Springs that gets up to 125 degrees in the summer to Chicago that gets below zero in the winter. I get the chills just thinking about it.

I will never forget the man that would inspire me while living in Chicago. Every day, in the afternoon, while walking to the train there was always a blind man rocking out on his keyboard. He was happy, had an AMAZING voice; he had soul and a great spirit. I could feel it. This man was BLIND. I would always ask myself, "Who helps him bring his keyboard, and two buckets down here every day?" This man never failed always to be there. He used one bucket as a stand for his keyboard and the other as a tip jar. He was like God, always present. He had so much life inside of him, so much soul, and he played that keyboard with all his heart as if it was the last day he was ever going to play. He inspired me, and he will never know it. I always made sure I tipped him. That was my way of showing him I appreciated him.

Many times seeing him would put things into perspective for me. Sometimes the radio business would get hectic and stressful, but seeing this man every day always reminded me to be thankful and grateful. He was my angel when I lived in Chicago. I wonder if he is still there?

As I was getting to LOVE Chicago, learning the streets, the highways, loving the people, visiting different suburbs, and of course enjoying the shopping down Michigan Ave, I made the decision that it was time to return home (Los Angeles) to continue to pursue bigger and greater things. Even though I did not have a clear plan, I did have a clear vision of how it was all going to unfold. I have always believed in the power of manifestation. Whatever you can see in your mind you can, without a doubt, manifest. But, you must believe in your vision 100 percent, even if no one else believes. What you think in your mind will manifest without a doubt. Just because your thoughts are silent, and no one can hear them does not mean they will not manifest.

I have heard my mentors say "when you are most uncomfortable is when you are growing the most." I was in a dilemma of loving the craft of radio, but not loving the format that I was working in. Talk about being out of your comfort zone. I was totally and completely out of my comfort zone. Good Lord! One of my mentors always reminds me that when you are in your comfort zone, you are not growing. With this in mind, I knew I was growing by leaps and bounds.

Something you need to understand about my move to Chicago is that it was completely unplanned. It happened all so quickly. I still remember the day my boss, at the time, offered me the job. He said, "I have a job offer for you in Chicago," I froze. Since my Spanish at the time was not that good, I could not even finish a Spanish sentence let alone rock a mic in Spanish, or so I thought. The company I was working at then only owned Spanish-speaking radio stations.

I was a bit shocked at his offer; I thought to myself, and the inner voice of self-doubt took over saying "your Spanish is not that good," and it wasn't. But, the beauty of life is that sometimes God sends people into your life that believe in you more than you believe in yourself. My boss, at that time, was one of those people. He saw in me something I did not see in myself. He believed that I could be a great co-host in Spanish radio. I just went with the flow feeling scared and a bit intimidated. But, I still went on and took the job.

Believe it or not, even though I felt scared and uncertain a part of my decision and the move felt right. I just knew something bigger was in store for me. I just had to believe and allow myself to go through this process.

After a good year in Chicago, suddenly things shifted, and I knew deep down inside it was time to leave. I have always believed I am guided. So, I listened to my inner voice a lot which to me is a characteristic of a true leader, a leader although scared still has to make important decisions.

The Inner Voice Never Lies

My inner voice was telling me, "Don't allow others including management to dictate your life and decisions." Management and people in powerful positions seem to think they know the answers to everything sometimes, but ONLY I knew the answer for me and what my heart truly wanted.

I have always understood ONE thing, that I AM IN CONTROL OF MY FUTURE.

I wanted to start relating to my audience and actually enjoy the music I was introducing on the radio. That just wasn't happening for me at the station I was at. I clearly remember my first live appearance at a club in Chicago. I was so out of place but had to pretend I was so excited to be there. I was far from excited. The radio station even took us shopping at a cowboy clothing store place. I thought free clothes YEEESSSS, NEVER imagining it was a western cowboy clothing store. I am not going to lie to you, the shopping in Chicago was AMAZING. Most of my check would go to shopping and living it up. I had no kids, no dependents, was a single girl, in a big city. My family and boyfriend at the time were thousands of miles away; I had to suck it up and make it work. Was the shopping I did the smartest thing? No! But, I learned my lesson and quickly stopped my crazy shopping habits.

The process was NOT easy! I was, all of a sudden, positioned to work with a co-host that I did not previously know. I just know he had a reputation for being crazy and impulsive. I THOUGHT to myself, "Fabulous we got something in common!" Two crazies in the morning, how the hell is this going to work? My co-host taught me so much about radio. Did I agree with everything he did? NO! But, I learned so much from him. Certain techniques and philosophies he applied to radio that were pretty amazing, so I became a sponge and started to absorb everything I was experiencing, learning and living. The good and the bad BRING IT ON. I was ready!

Ever since I was a little girl, I always have been a LEADER. I grew up in a middle-class family as the baby; my dad was a construction worker, and my mom worked in corporate America. She was stressed 24/7. I still remember her coming home as a stress ball every day crying, breaking out on her face due to stress and being moody; it was crazy because she did not know how to balance her life. I tend to think this is part of the reason why BALANCE is so important to me now, and I strive for it every day because I consciously do not want to repeat that cycle. My parents taught my brother, sister and me to be independent from a young age. I am so thankful for that. They had a rule that if we wanted a car at 16 years old, we had to pay for our own car insurance. I thought that was pretty fair. It taught us responsibility. My brother, sister and I all had jobs by the time we were 16. My first job was at Walmart, and I remember reading a quote somewhere that truly stuck with me, it said: "Whatever you do, do it with all your heart," that is exactly what I did at Walmart. I became the best cart pusher, and I would turn it into fun. I would compete with the other guys who did the same job as me and in turn, I would create the fun for all of us.

My parents were not the type to enable their kids; they actually lit a fire underneath our asses to do something with our lives. By the end of my high school days, my dad was on my ass asking me what my plans were next. He told me *"you either work or get into college because I do not believe in breaks, a break will lead you to become lazy, and we do not do lazy in this family."* Clearly, even if I wanted a break, it was not going to happen. At 19 I moved out of my house to live with my first boyfriend, talk about independence. My dad was not the happiest with my decision of moving out, but I still did it. It was my life, my journey and I did not care who approved or not. I had the best intention with my life when I moved out, and I reassured my dad of that, he still wasn't convinced, but I did it anyway.

"No one knows what's best for you but you. Of course, listening to your elders who have been there, done that, is great; but you still need to live your journey and go through your own lessons."

I have always been a rebel when it comes to my life and my decisions because I know that I am blessed and guided. Even if I get lost on the journey sometimes, which is ok, I will always find my way back. I feel that when you get lost or off-track a little bit, it is because you have lessons to learn, and unless you go through those detours, the lessons will not be learned. Enjoy the detours.

My Faith Foundation

This faith foundation comes from years of being involved in church a lot. I grew up a Catholic girl; I even went to private Catholic School growing up. I loved it because I did not have to pick and choose what I was going to wear to school because I wore the same uniform every day. I am not a practicing Catholic now, but I do have an amazing relationship with God. We talk every day, and I know He has my back. So, being the baby of the family, I always wanted to tag along everywhere, so I became the leader of the youth group. I was in the church choir, and we sang on Saturday and Sunday and believe it or not I even served as an altar server. *I got fired from that position because the priest caught me eating the Eucharist.* Only the priest is supposed to open the tabernacle, and he caught me opening it and chomping on what many call a symbolism of "the body of Christ." I loved the taste of those little breads. I am telling you I am a natural born rebel with a cause.

As the youth group leader, I would step up to the plate all the time. I was not afraid to speak in a microphone, lead a crowd, lead in prayer, put my hand up, say my name loud and proud. I have known from a young age that God was going to use me to touch millions of lives, some people I know and some people I do not know. This experience of being a leader at our youth group I believe allowed me to develop my gift that I have with people. The gift of connection and real conversation will never get old. True connection is what I live for.

My mom told me an awesome story a few years ago as we were conversing about back when we were really involved in the church. She said there was an intense prayer session going on and I was all up in the mix. I would feel it because prayer is energy. Everything is energy. And, I guess the prayer was so intense that I fainted in what she called "the holy spirit." YES, I had "fainted in the Holy Spirit," so it was a peaceful faint. I was somewhat asleep in a peaceful way so my mom was not worried because it would happen to people, every so often, and you just have to let them rest, so that is what they did to me, they let me rest. I woke up like 5 minutes after and my mom just hugged me and told me I was special because I had fainted in the Holy Spirit. Guess what? I chose to believe I am special so therefore I AM.

"What you believe the truth for yourself to be, it will be!"

Parents, if you have children uplift them with your words. You can make or break them. I was lucky enough to have parents who really uplifted my brother, sister and me with their words. They would feed us a lot of hard love, but it was always with the intention of seeing us grow, blossom and win. Little did they know they were creating a leader in me.

Tough Love Is What I Needed

A bold, fearless, unafraid to speak my mind, leader is what my parents helped me believe I could be. But, besides my parents I had other people help mold the person I have now become. At just the tender age of 20 years old I landed an opportunity to do radio in Palm Springs at a station called U92.7 the hip-hop station of the desert. We would reach cities like Indio, Coachella, Desert Hot Springs and others. This was my first radio job that I had landed based on a recommendation from someone that I had interned with before. I had to make it down to Palm Springs in a matter of 3 weeks. I hauled ass, acted quick, found a place to live without even giving myself the chance to think twice. This felt so right, scary as hell, but so right. I was OFFICIALLY going to be on the radio for the first time. Everything about this opportunity felt surreal. This is what I had worked for, interned for, went to school for, and BOOM before you know it I was in Palm Springs living in the back house of a house that was under construction ... FEARLESS. I had to get up every morning with the full intention of perfecting my craft -- radio. I clearly had never done this before, so my delivery was not where it needed to be. I sounded like a robot on the radio it was hard for me to let loose at the beginning of my radio days. It was hard to be me.

"So many times we hold back from who we really are, not realizing that being who we fully are is everything. This is why people fall in love with you."

My program director aka "The Boss" hot-lined me a few times. In radio terms, when someone hotlines you on the internal line, you better pick up. So I picked up one time, and he basically ripped me a new asshole. He was like "RaqC, what type of delivery was that? It sounded like you were reading off a piece of paper!" which I was. He went on to say "I hired you because I believed in you and that BIG personality of yours not to sound like a regular boring reporter, you have that BIG personality that's why I hired you, so use it!" He basically put me in my place in a very tough love sort of way. What I did back in those days, since I was clueless as to what I was doing, is I would deliver the entertainment report verbatim.

Back then, when I was new to the radio business, I could not understand the concept of separating business from personal. So every time he brought to my attention my delivery style, I would take it personally and I felt he was picking on me, BUT he wasn't. He was actually giving me constructive criticism; he only wanted me to be the very best I could be. I could not even see that. This battle with him and I went on for a while until I finally started to understand him as a leader. He knew his vision, and he knew my potential, just like I knew my vision when taking this job of becoming a radio personality and learning the craft of radio. I thank God for mentors and coaches like him in my life because they help you sometimes see what you cannot otherwise see in yourself. To this day I am super thankful for him, my first radio boss. He taught me valuable lessons that I will take with me forever. He believed in me from the jump, and he knew I had what it took.

Along my journey there have been more than people doubting me, it has been more of me self-doubting myself. Like I said at the beginning of my chapter only some have the courage to talk about it. Along the ways I have had relationships that have made me second guess an opportunity; I have had money situations make me second guess opportunities. But, nothing is more powerful than you doubting yourself. As a leader who understands:

"to whom much is given, much is expected," I have always felt that I will have more trials and tribulations than the average person because I am here to teach through my own experiences and give hope. I believe that is indeed the case in all leaders that have ever existed.

In Palm Springs, I was working two jobs to make ends meet. I was not making enough at the radio station to maintain my life, so I was working part-time at the radio station and part-time at Smart & Final. At Smart & Final, I was a cashier. I was a damn good one too. I put my heart into everything I do. People would wait in long lines just to make sure I would check them out through my line. My gift with people has always been that I connect. I genuinely do and don't mind it at all. I learn from everyone that crosses my path. I learn many times what I do not want to be or what I want to be more of.

People would constantly ask me, "Are you the girl from the radio?" I would deny it. I was ashamed and embarrassed. Embarrassed and afraid of what people were going to think of me working as a cashier until I realized they were not paying my bills. The giving a shit did not last too long. I got over that really quickly, but I must admit it was a struggle. Looking back in retrospect, I know what made me different was the fact after I had gotten over caring, I was really free. My biggest lesson from this whole experience is never be ashamed of where you come from or what you have had to do to get to where you are now or where you want to be.

I like to say that I am a cycle-breaker in my family. From a young age, I have always been pretty defined and observant. I think I have adapted the free spirit vibe not only because I feel like a hippie and should have been born in the 70's but because that is what I have been allowed to be since I was a young girl. I have learned from the mistakes or successes of others, and I either repeat the good or don't repeat the bad. I believe there is major power in breaking family cycles of bullshit, and everyone can do it, but most think it is hard. Habit and long lines of generational cycles will sometimes trick us to believe it cannot be done but it sure can. When you break a cycle, you are basically re-creating something from scratch. That is powerful. That is what a leader does.

From a young age I started going to 12-step programs, and I learned very early on a mantra that says, "take what you like and leave the rest!" In other words take what you like from any situation, conversation, book, business deal, and leave what you did not like behind. Don't judge it, just leave it behind.

Leaving things behind can be very challenging sometimes, but it is a quality a good leader possesses. Sometimes despite the pain, it must happen. The thought of leaving things behind is scary. Relationships, jobs, friendships, old eating habits, old routines, etc. We become creatures of habit. We do what we know how to do day in and day out. Evolution is beautiful when embraced.

To evolve into a new person is success. To evolve in a career is magic. To be unafraid to do it is priceless.

I have always known that in order to be a leader you must possess some type of magic. You must recognize your gifts, talents, and uniqueness. Everyone can be a leader, but many don't realize their greatness, and it is easier to be a follower. I recognized my magic, and it began at a young age. I woke up to my greatness, to my ability to first inspire myself then inspire others. I have always believed a true leader creates other leaders, and I get such joy out of that. I call it living my life with purpose. Are you living your life with purpose? If not, NOW IS THE TIME!

Dedication

It is with the most utmost gratitude that I thank God for this opportunity! My great grandma Mama Matty for being such a big influence in my life. My family: Mom, Daddy, Susie, and Joe you guys are my rocks and you all fill my soul. To the people that tried to keep me in a box thank you for showing me my true power. My 4th grade teacher Mrs. Karen Podgorski you taught me that I had a voice. Thank you I am forever thankful. To my ride or die's, my REAL friends, your love and support are EPIC in my world and to all the beautiful souls in the world that support me, whether we have met or not I appreciate you and love you more than you will ever know. *Mil Gracias*!

Biography

Raquel "RaqC" Cordova

Radio/TV Personality, Motivational Speaker, Philanthropist and Social Media Influencer.

Raquel Cordova, better known as RaqC, originates from Riverside, CA. Her radio career began in 2000 at U-92.7 in Palm Springs as the morning show co-host. Shorty after, Spanish Broadcasting System, Inc. (SBS) came calling & RaqC accepted an on-air position with the regional Mexican station, La Ley 107.9 in Chicago. Her successful run in Chicago gave her the experience to master the art of radio as well as fine-tune her second language, Spanish.

When hearing that a station in Los Angeles was being restructured to a bilingual format she took the risk and left Chicago determined to become a permanent voice in Los Angeles. It was worth the risk. RaqC enjoyed a successful 8-year run with Latino 96.3fm becoming the top personality for the station. She went on to entertain Los Angelinos on their afternoon drive home with Exitos 93.9fm and most recently was the co-host of "The "RaqC and Nachin Show" on the newly branded Mega 96.3fm.

RaqC credits her free spirit as the inspiration to seize every opportunity that presents itself. She views radio as an outlet to express her love, happiness, and ambitions with the masses. Her passions include music, representing

Latino culture in a positive light, and sharing her stories of success to motivate others. RaqC has even ventured into the world of TV as one of the 2011 Mun2 reality show stars on "Jenni Rivera Presents: Chiquis and RaqC".

La Opinion coined RaqC "The Queen of Spanglish Media" as her career spans from radio to TV to red carpet coverage to blogging for Latina Magazine and as a result has now been identified as a social media influencer by some of our favorite brands (*AT&T, McDonalds, Pepsi, Alma Awards, T-Mobile, Latina Magazine, All-State, Bud Light, GOT Milk CA Campaign, NBC Universo, Universal Music Group, Dr. Boris, Terranea Resort, Diablo Pops, El Silencio Mezcal, Mun2 and Buick*)

Embracing the influence she has on others coupled with her spirit of giving, RaqC founded Amigas4MySoul, a non-profit organization established to promote unity and empowerment among women. In addition, RaqC is known as a motivational speaker, having addressed crowds of a few thousand at several Universities in the Los Angeles area and is known for inspiring other young Latinas to pursue their dreams. To top it all off she created "Brazen by RaqC" which is a lifestyle brand featuring unique clothing, hats, sunglasses that represent the essence of who she is. The word Brazen means Bold, Shameless & Unapologetic! It's no surprise RaqC has created a brand with a mission to teach people to Live with no regrets and Be Brazen! Shop for the latest Brazen t-shirts and hats at http://www.brazenbyraqc.com

RaqC was voted one of La Opinion's 2013 Mujeres Destacadas Award Winner in the category of Arts and Culture and a Latina of Influence by Hispanic Lifestyle. In 2015 she was voted Best Radio DJ Personality by Latin Mixx and was chosen as Alegria Magazine's Inspirational Award Winner.

CHAPTER TWO

Guts & Grace

The Realization

I take a deep breath as I shuffle through my notes for the hockey player interview I am about to do and make sure my cameraman and microphone are waiting in the wings ready to sprint for the locker room as soon as we get the cue. As the locker room doors swing open, and the herd of reporters stampedes their way in, I muscle my way through the crowd to make sure I can get my microphone in the face of the star player to ensure I get the best audio. This usually isn't that hard because of my 5'2 frame. With the all the chaos, sweat, and stress, I have never made it a point to make out the faces in the sea of reporters. All I ever focused on was my interview questions, composure, and execution but this time, it was different. I turn my head and notice that I am the only woman reporter at this very moment and for the first time I felt like time stood still. I took a deep breath as I was able to capture this moment and for the very first time in my sports broadcasting career, I said to myself, "Wow, this is special, and I am so thankful for the path that brought me here!"

The Beginning

Did I grow up thinking I was going to lead, or believe that I was going to be a broadcaster influencing the tide in any way? No, I just knew, at a very early age, that I had an obsession with the arts, and I did not want to miss any news broadcast because I was captivated by the news anchors. I had no idea that my multi-faceted passion for entertainment would become a platform where I would speak to people on how to make their dreams a reality. The only thing I was certain about growing up is that nothing was going to stop me from dreaming and accomplishing what my family worked so hard to achieve. I give my parents all the credit in the world for giving me the opportunities that led to where I am today. I was born in Armenia, Colombia and when I was six months old, they decided to move to the United States. Of course, this story echoes among many immigrant families searching for a better life. My parents did just that, and they are the example of hard work achieving the American Dream. They taught me at a very early age that hard work, honesty, and patience pays off even if, at the moment, it may not feel or look like it. But, most of all they taught me to dream and dream big.

Breaking Into The Business

Many people ask me how I broke into the world of entertainment and sports broadcasting. And, it always makes me pause because my story is a roller coaster and not linear; but that is what I love. I have never wanted to be defined by one thing and have tried many different avenues because I have always been a restless spirit. I guess that is why I was nicknamed Media-Gypsy, but I will get to that later.

I always knew one thing, though; I had a passion for people, and I knew I wanted to make a difference.

I grew up taking dance classes, and my parents always encouraged me to be ambitious even though some of my projects seem less than conventional. From being a professional salsa dancer to cheering for the NFL Miami Dolphins, modeling, being a food stylist, party starter, radio personality, choreographer, producer, production assistant and the list goes on and on, trust me, there were moments where I was like, "Is this my life?"

It is hard to find stability when you are juggling different jobs to pay the bills so that you can chase your dreams. I got a great opportunity when I was hired to intern for NBC 6. From there, I realized that it was going to take long hours with no pay to just get the experience needed to get the broadcasting job I wanted. I worked endless reporter jobs, for no money, but I knew I had to get the experience. For years I took all the jobs that came my way, some glamorous some not so glamorous. There were times where I doubted myself and didn't know where it was all going. And, many doubters had less than encouraging words. Although, traditional news was an option, at that point in my life I did not want to go that route. I wanted to focus on producing and try to land an entertainment reporter job, which is a job that everyone and their grandmother is after.

I was told I was too short; I did not have enough experience, that I did not fit the mold, whatever that meant. But, the more I kept on getting rejected, the more fire and drive I built within me; I knew I was not going to be deterred by anyone. I am not going to lie; my parents were always worried because there was no rhyme or reason to what I was doing, but they always let me do my thing and encouraged me lovingly along the way.

Important Questions

I had to ask myself who was I going to be in this world and what was I made of? There were endless nights where doubt tried to creep in, and moments where I too was falling prey to the naysayers. Don't get me wrong; I was building a body of work and a name for myself without even knowing it. I had booked national modeling campaigns, reported on glamorous red carpets, danced on international stages, but the nature of it all still brought me back to the same question, "whom did I want to be?" Working freelance is exciting, but the instability of it all wears on you.

Slowly but surely I was becoming a Jack of All Trades, Master of None, which in my case was not such a bad thing, but I did not know that at the time.

I truly believe everything happens for a reason, and I can remember the moment my life took a turn and defined my trajectory and how I broke into the world of sports reporting.

I was at an NHL Florida Panthers game with my dad and saw a female broadcaster on the big screen making fans laugh and entertaining the arena. I looked over to my dad and said to him, "That's the job I want!" Before I knew it, I was making calls, sending resumes and trying to get my foot in the door. When I finally was able to speak to a decision-maker, I got rejected. After being deflated by the rejection, I decided to immerse myself in the world of sports and ever since cheering for the NFL, I had made contacts that would help me along the way. But, one thing I continued to do was submit my information to the Florida Panthers, until years later, guess what? I got a call from the Panthers about wanting to hire me as their arena host and digital reporter. I guess persistence does pay off!

Hockey In South Florida

I worked for the team for four seasons and during my time there different sports media outlets started to hire me. Little-by-little, I earned a name for myself as a sports media personality, which is something I never set out to do. What I did set out to do was seize opportunities even if it was dressed up in overalls and looked like serious work. I was given a unique opportunity with the Florida Panthers during my fourth season. I not only was the arena host and digital reporter but I was given the opportunity to be Latin Marketing Manager. This meant that everything I did in English I was going to do in Spanish.

It gave me the chance to speak Spanish to educate the South Florida community about hockey, which was no easy feat. It positioned me as the bilingual spokesperson for the franchise and gave me the opportunity to spearhead marketing initiatives that would capture the Hispanic market. This meant trying to convince people, in a boardroom, to stand behind my ideas even if they did not understand. Was there doubt on my end?, Of course, but I knew I had to follow my gut instinct. It all seemed pretty bold, when I look back, considering that there was a lot riding on me. But, if you are not going to bet on yourself who will? I was proud to receive the South Florida Communications Leadership Award for my outreach efforts, an award I humbly accepted, and of course made my parents proud.

Throughout my sports entertainment career, I kept on noticing that there was a lack of women in the industry. In the last ten years, women have made great strides to be an important part of the sports world but from what I noticed we still have a long way to go.

Charting Tricky Waters

What I do know is that if we are going to chart the waters of the sports and the entertainment world, we better do it with class, dignity, and have a serious work ethic. I say this because it just takes a couple of bad apples to ruin it for the rest of us. I have noticed that although men and women are on the same playing field, I cannot help but realize that we are held to a higher standard. I am passionate about women in sports and speak at conferences about breaking into the world of broadcasting, and how important branding and marketing play in this digital world. I receive messages, from men and women alike, asking me how I made it happen for myself? Little did I know I was influencing young college students who were just like me when I started. But, the difference is that I never had anyone to show me the way.

I always say if I can do it, you can do it. My fourth year of working for the Florida Panthers came to an end when I got an opportunity to work the WWE/NXT as a TV host and ring announcer, a coveted role I never imaged would come my way. I am currently traveling the world doing what I love. Although I would never have guessed that I would be working for a world-renowned company like the WWE, I do know that all my decisions led me to where I am.

Game Changer

Many people ask me if I have always been successful in the entertainment industry. The answer to that is, "no." Some years were good; other years were great, and there were some that I am happy are over. One of the things that I like to highlight is that my career started to shift in a positive direction when I started to think like a business person. I always wanted to blog, and it took a long time to find the courage to put my thoughts out there for everyone to read. I created Media-Gypsy, Entertainment for the Wandering Soul. Media-Gypsy is a blog about career advice, candid moments, lifestyle tips, behind the scenes, and more. I always considered myself an artist, never did I consider myself a business woman. I did not know anything about launching a business, or how to create a sustainable income from something I created but little by little I learned how to make money blogging, and before I knew it, I had a business on my hands.

I learned the importance of educating yourself regarding the business side of things. By combining business with my artsy side, I was able to turn my ideas into opportunities. I cannot stress enough the importance of taking a look at your talents to see how you can create a sustainable business model, and be able to find the freedom to work on the projects you love. I wish I would have done this earlier in my career because as soon as I was able to think like a business woman the faster I was taken seriously and not just looked upon as talent. There's nothing wrong with being talent, but there's power in knowing the industry's business side of the projects that you are involved with, and it makes you more valuable.

Be The Role Model You Always Needed

In our journey, we may stumble and fall, and that is the beauty of it all. But, there are things that we can control. We cannot control outside factors, but we can control how we react to certain situations and how we position ourselves for others to notice us. To stand out from the crowd, there are certain decisions we need to make about how we want to be perceived. From the way we dress, our social media and branding. What we put out there lasts forever and has long term consequences if you are not careful with what you are posting about yourself. An Instagram post speaks a thousand words; Facebook posts can get you fired, and Tweets can make you Internet famous or infamous. I always say to young girls to think about their bigger picture and try to see beyond the instant gratification of social media posts. I use the rule of thumb: if I have to think twice about whether this post will be taken out of context, I do not post. I also ask myself, "What would my parents think?" That usually is a good barometer to see whether something is SnapChat, Instagram or Twitter worthy. *Ladies, no more Instagram duck faces while you pose in your underwear with the toilet seat behind you.* If you want to be a model, do it and become a business. You will thank yourself later.

Believing

If you want to accomplish great things you, must believe in yourself even when others do not believe in you. Of course, you are going to get strangers who will doubt you and perhaps laugh at you. But, how about when your family or loved ones have trouble understanding your dreams and what you want to do? Chase your dreams anyway. It is ok if they do not understand you. All they have to do is love you and little-by-little they will see your drive and get behind you. But before others believe in your dreams, you have to believe in yourself first. You have to become your biggest fan because no one is going to be convinced and follow suit if you are not 100% committed to making things happen.

Branding

Regardless what your goals may be, or what you want to ultimately do in life, it is important to stand out from the crowd. Since we live in a digital world, aesthetics and design play a big role in how we are perceived. They say a picture speaks a thousand words, and your brand is no different. I suggest a visual presence, whether a website, logo, business cards, headshots and so forth. There are many times I run into people that don't have business cards or a website, and this could potentially be a missed opportunity. People ask me how to get started with creating a brand and that is a loaded question because it depends on what your goal is. I would ask you, "What do you want to convey, and how do I want to do it visually?" This is a lot of fun because you are the master of your message and are limitless regarding your brand and its message.

Making A Plan

How are you going to arrive at your destination without a map? When I was working gig to gig, looking back, I realized that I was aimlessly wandering hoping to land my dream job. Although it was rational at the time, I see where rubbing a lucky rabbits foot and putting all my eggs in one basket called chance was a bit silly. Things started to click for me when I got very specific in regards to what I wanted to achieve in my career, and I was very detailed in describing what that looked like. Remember that everyone's version of success looks very different, so you have to figure out what success looks like to you.

I created the dream scenario about where I wanted to land my hosting career, what my blog looked like, and all the dream content I wished to use. I wrote down where I wanted to do my public speaking engagements, and created an outline describing what my dream client looked like. My map showed my bigger picture. No goal was too big, and no idea was too small. Once I created my larger than life dream map, I figure out the steps I needed to take to achieve each particular goal. This took a long time and research, but once it was done, I had a step-by-step guide to achieving my dreams.

Work Ethic

It was always important to understand what my non-negotiables were when working with projects and people from every walk of life. At an early age, I prescribed to a work philosophy that never steered me wrong, thanks to my parents. Accountability, kindness, leading by example, and grace have always been a part of my foundation. These are important for when I have to draw a line in the sand and make tough decisions. I find that being accountable, although challenging at times, is the best thing that one can do because it personally gives me satisfaction in moving a situation forward. I learned at an early age that kindness could get you far, regardless if it is being kind to someone that cannot do anything for you. I have always learned the best way to lead is by example, and I learned at a very young age that someone is always watching.

What better way to lead than to show that you are authentic in your beliefs. Once you show authenticity, people will see that you are the real deal that walks the walk. Maneuvering stressful situations can be a bit tricky, but showing grace under fire can help you sustain the mental clarity you need to face any adversity. Showing a strong work ethic can catapult you and sustain your dream by paving the road for others to follow.

Never Take No For Answer

What happens when someone slams a door in your face? When I say slam, I am referring to rejection. If the door slams shut, try the next door. Although rejection feels horrible and can even lead to questioning the very fiber of your existence, you just have to keep on going. In a sea of no's it only takes a yes to change your course direction and make a difference placing you on the path to where you were meant to be. In my journey, I have heard all the reasons in the world to why I did not get the job. I was too short, I did not have the right hair color, I was too animated, blah, blah, blah. I have heard it all before, and I am not going to lie to you and say that it was easy to hear it all. There were times that it ruined my day; then, I went home and ate chocolate chip cookies. But, the very next day I was back at it again, even more determined than ever. I always say, "It is okay to sulk and even feel depressed about a certain situation, just don't unpack your bags there." I prescribe to that philosophy and make sure never to unpack my bags when things get tough.

Surround Yourself with the People That Get It

When you are pursuing your bliss, it can be difficult to find a tribe or even one person that gets it. It has been a lifelong challenge for me to find people who get the industry I work in. People can be interested in what you do but not ever get it and that's ok. But when you find people that get it, hold on tight to them because they are the people who become the friends who give you the encouragement and the fire you need when you are looking for a push. There have been numerous times when the world had me down and was questioning every decision I was making, but my circle of friends helped me through and gave me the nudge I needed to get re-energized. Without them who knows if I would have been able to find the spark to continue vigorously on my journey.

Follow In The Pursuit of Your Dreams

Regardless what you do in life, do it with passion. Don't allow fear to dictate your direction or deter you from following what you always wanted to do. I regularly get asked if I ever was afraid to put myself out there for the world to judge? And, the answer is yes. Originally I was terrified to put myself out there, but I pushed forward despite the fear. I no longer feel scared to live out what I was set out to do. I do often feel butterflies right before going on stage or right before I hit publish. I think I will feel the butterflies and use them to be the best entertainer/reporter/writer I can be. My last morsel of advice is to pursue your passion despite the challenges you may face. You may feel doubt, and you may not know where to start, but the most important thing is just to start. You will face adversity and bumps in the road, but trust your gut feeling and remember that with guts and grace anything is possible!

Dedication

I would like to thank my parents, Aura & Mario Ocampo for always believing in me and for pushing me to be the best version of myself. I'm grateful to my fellow co-workers past and present for their encouragement and continued inspiration.

Biography

Andrea Ocampo is a bilingual sports, entertainment, and lifestyle television host as well as an accomplished speaker, blogger, and producer. Experienced in a variety of genres, she's currently trailblazing the sports/entertainment broadcasting industry leaving a lasting impression on fans everywhere. Her electric personality made her a fan favorite and could be seen at the NHL's Florida Panthers, FAU Football, and ESPN's Marmot Boca Raton Bowl. It was easy to see why Ocampo was a fan favorite. She has been featured on ESPN and Fox Sports talking about the latest sports news as both an anchor and a sideline reporter. She's also served as the public address announcer for the 2015 NHL Draft and was the first Spanish speaking female public address announcer in the NHL. Most recently, she was hired by WWE/NXT to be their latest ring announcer/host under the name Andrea D'Marco.

Enter, Stage Left

A self-titled chameleon in the business, Ocampo's journey began in Armenia, Colombia. Shortly after her birth, her family moved to South Florida in search of a better life. It was then that Ocampo showed her first signs of a love for entertainment. Enrolled in dance classes at an early age, Ocampo's life has always involved performing.

"As a kid, just about my favorite thing to do after school was put on a pair of ridiculously high leather boots, smear my mom's red lipstick on, and dance to Vanilla Ice's 'Ice Ice Baby' in front of the mirror," recalls Ocampo. "A few years later, I traded in my hairbrush for a real microphone, earned a degree in broadcasting, and started living my dream."

A Jack Of All Trades

During the off-season Ocampo's talents are widely sought after in the world of entertainment and lifestyle, with many national television shows to her name. She recently wrapped a travel series for the Walt Disney Company where both she and Mickey Mouse take you through the various activities available while visiting the company's Orlando theme parks. She'll also be making an appearance on the Travel Channel as she goes on an unforgettable adventure to Greece on the upcoming show "One Way

Ticket". Experienced in digital media in a variety of formats, Ocampo has covered prestigious red carpet events, including being featured as an entertainment expert on "CNN En Español", Yahoo!, CBS, and others. Thanks to her overwhelming versatility in everything from cars to sports, pop culture, health, travel, and fitness, it's no wonder Andrea has been nicknamed the Media-Gypsy.

Social Impact & Women Empowerment

When she's not in front of the camera, Ocampo is a popular public speaker at colleges and social media conferences, due in part to her unique perspective regarding women and their ever-growing presence in the worlds of sports, multimedia, branding, and content creation.

Through Media-Gypsy.com, Ocampo constantly strives to inspire, encourage, and motivate those who are seeking to build their brand and find their voice, helping others become an influence in their respective industries through her lifestyle blog and talent-coaching business.

The 5' 2", Ocampo has proved that this talented and versatile Latina continues to become a woman of influence, proving that there are no boundaries where media meets business, and that Andrea is here to stay.

Furthering her ever growing umbrella of media savvy, Ocampo is a guest writer for Hoy En Tec, Recruiter Magazine, and Miami Social Magazine, where she lends her perspective about business, marketing, and digital marketing trends. She's also a member of the National Association of Hispanic Journalists, Association for Women in Sports Media, and the Barry University Sport Management Advisory Board. Most recently she oversaw digital and content creation for Palm Beach Broadcasting, a cluster of seven radio stations in the ever growing and diverse South Florida market.

Andrea Ocampo is a Colombian, bilingual sports, entertainment, and lifestyle television host. Experienced in a variety of genres, she's currently trailblazing the media industry. She has been featured on ESPN, Fox Sports, CNN Español, Yahoo!, CBS, Univision and was the arena host/reporter for the NHL Florida Panthers where she became a fan favorite. Most recently she was hired by the WWE/NXT to be a host, an opportunity that has catapulted her to international notoriety.

When she's not in front of the camera, Ocampo is a sought after public speaker at colleges and media conferences, due in part to her unique perspective regarding women and their ever-growing presence in the world of sports. Through her lifestyle blog Media-Gypsy she strives to inspire, and empower women who are seeking to build their brand and find their voice. Through her ever constant drive and passion, Ocampo continues to live out her life motto "With guts and grace, anything is possible!".

A Vibrant Future

What's on the horizon for Andrea?

Soon she will be launching her, "Morning Coffee" video series on her lifestyle blog. Through this program, Ocampo hopes to give a bit of inspiration to women in business, or anyone looking for a little encouragement. She's also launching online coaching programs to reach those that can't attend her lectures in person. Through her ever constant drive and passion, Andrea Ocampo continues to live out her life motto "With guts and grace, anything is possible!," combining her quirky, fun, and lovable girl next door attitude with professionalism and ethical journalism.

CHAPTER THREE

This I Know For Sure

"A mind, once expanded by a new idea,
never returns to its original dimensions."

–Oliver Wendell Holmes Sr.

When I was asked to be a participating author for this book, I caught myself wondering how much value I could truly be able to provide for you in just one chapter. One thing I have learned through all my years is that being of value first is memorable to people. Introspectively, I started mulling over all that I have learned, the books I have read and the people that I have met. I believe that within these pages lie the fundamental truths for how I operate each day. Am I perfect at following all of the leadership habits and attributes included here?

Hell no! However, what I have witnessed is that people who do operate with these philosophies in mind achieve success in their personal and professional lives. They are true leaders.

The question of whether you are born a leader or can develop into a leader is highly debated. Was I born a leader? No, I was not. Maybe it is because I did not come from a family of leaders. I believe that leadership awareness is a skill that I have developed over time. The starting point of any developed attribute is unique to the awareness you have of it. I believe it is not the school that you went to, the degrees obtained or the career titles that have been bestowed upon you. What I can share, is that leadership is sometimes thankless but when done right can be incredibly rewarding once you understand that true leadership comes with a great deal of risk. Whether you are searching for leadership lessons for your career or your personal life, much of what you will read here will apply to both. What I am sharing here within this passage are the goods on leadership and the challenges of leadership. That way, you have the full perspective, according to the *Book of Patty*.

First, what qualifies me to write about leadership you ask? Well, my journey has been one of professional and personal leadership development. The following include lessons learned along the way so that I can save you time, effort, money and pain.

Leaders Take Responsibility For Their Results (Good Or Bad)

I come from a blue-collar family and I am very proud of that. My dad was a car painter and my mom, a factory worker. They were hard workers and always provided for my brother and me. What they most wanted for us was a formal education and for both of us to have a good career, especially since they did not have those opportunities in Central America. Looking back, I was so programmed to understand that after high school, I would go to college. My father's biggest wish was for me to find a white collar job, get a door (aka an office), a nice car and a cell phone. Naturally, I wanted to make my parents proud, so I had my marching orders and moved through their plan for my success. I didn't believe anything else was possible.

Here's the thing, life lessons are truly intended to help mold who you become, but it's up to you whether it defines you or empowers you. Let me explain, I attended an all-girl private Catholic high school and at the time, this was a big stretch for my parents financially. I wore the standard uniform skirt, white shirts, cardigan sweaters and knock off penny loafers. I quickly noticed that the popular girls wore Polo sweaters, a status symbol (or so I believed at the time). I wanted one of those sweaters bad… really bad. So for Christmas, I asked my mom for nothing more than a Polo cardigan. Christmas day came, and my mom proudly presented a beautifully wrapped box to me, I was giddy with Christmas joy; I knew that the sacred sweater I had longed for was finally within my reach. I tore through the box as quickly as possible and much to my surprise it was a *Hunt Club from JC Penney* cardigan. I was mortified and acted like a complete teenage drama queen about it, "I can't wear *this*… it is JC Penney, *not* a Polo cardigan!" Let me paint the picture: here's my mom, a factory worker making just above minimum wage and with much sacrifice, buying a gift for me. And, as she saw the disgusted look on my face, she was not only shocked at my lack of gratitude but appalled at my behavior. Now those who know my mom know that she can go from zero to one-hundred on the pissed off chart, you can definitely call her a fiery Latina mom. She firmly stated, "this is what we can afford, those Polo sweaters cost $50… I don't wear Polo sweaters and I have a job! You want a Polo sweater?… YOU go get a job!" And, she yanked the box from my hands, mumbled a litany of swear words in Spanish about what an ingrate I was and stormed out of the room. I had realized how much I had hurt my mother and so rudely rejected her act of kindness. I did get a job in high school, actually often had two jobs to afford whatever I wanted within the limits of what I could earn, at $3.65 per hour minimum wage at the time. That was the starting point of my journey into the workforce.

I am thankful for that very important lesson for so many reasons. It helped me to realize that I had to take 100% responsibility for my actions. It's called cause and effect. In essence, leadership is no different. Just because you have a big title or a swanky position at a job or you are a business owner, does not mean you get to pick and choose situations and they will always be in your favor. You have to take 100% responsibility for that title and the results you attain from it, good or bad. It's called total responsibility and it applies to both your personal life as well as your professional life. I always marvel when people blame others for their results in life. Leaders understand that personal accountability is part of the leadership equation. You want different results in your life? Then it's up to you and only you to make them happens. This reminds me of Jim Rohn's, the late business philosopher, brilliant quote, "leadership is the challenge to be something more than average." That has been my mantra for a long time, no matter how many times I fall, no matter how many times I fail, I remember this important concept. Understand cause and effect. Take 100% responsibility for your results, it really does provide peace of mind because it allows you to look within to understand the feedback and do better next time.

Leaders "Zag."

I learned my strong work ethic from my parents working throughout my high school and college years. Perhaps this comes from an immigrant mentality, but my parents always told me to work very hard if I wanted to succeed. Later in life I realized that yes, a work ethic is important, but working smarter is even better. I did not go to an Ivy League school, but what I lack in pedigree I make up in energy and grit. When I graduated from college, quite honestly, I had a difficult time finding a job. I would apply for many jobs and then play the waiting game with no forward movement. Clearly, this approach was not working. I felt idle and uninspired.

I had an epiphany one day when I went personally to apply for a job and upon submitting my application and resume, I noticed that the Human Resources woman placed it on a pile of other applications. Holy cow! *How was I supposed to stand out from that pile?*

Looking at that pile made me realize that there was no way for me to feasibly stand out from the crowd, I was just another application. So after thinking it through a bit, I figured that I had to include something above and beyond just the application. Something that really could could garner the attention of the hiring manager. What I started doing was not only applying for work, but I would include in my cover letter an "irresistible offer". I would offer the hiring manager to work for absolutely free for one month so that the company could "test" me out. I figured that was a win/win; I would get in front of the right people and they would get free labor. Sure, I was taking on all the risk, but I figured I could just waitress at night while I worked during the day. One privately owned company took me up on my "work for free" offer and after three weeks of free labor, they hired me as an Account Executive.

I learned that just doing what everybody else was doing isn't enough. It does not stand out. Quite frankly it is mediocre. There's a great branding book called, *Zag* by Marty Neumeier where he challenges his reader to "zag" which means to basically BE DIFFERENT. That is how you stand out. He says that when everyone else is "zigging," you have to "zag." And, that's why I got the job, not because I filled out the application. I simply "zagged" when everyone on that pile of applications was "zigging." It is a great strategy that has worked well for me throughout my professional career. I've used the concept of zagging over and over, it definitely works. It is also a strategy that has helped within my entrepreneurial career. It shows gumption, action and being a risk taker. Remember when everyone else is zigging, you must zag. Marty knows best on this one.

Leaders Challenge Conventional Wisdom And Back It Up.

I spent over fifteen years in Corporate America. Over that tenure, I worked under many titled leaders such as CEO, COO, etc. I also worked with direct managers where most of them were managers and in a couple of cases, leaders. Managers follow orders; leaders challenge conventional wisdom. Managers will work toward meeting business objectives; leaders will question why you are going that way in the first place and offer an alternative path driven by justification, not just an opinion.

What sets apart the progressive leader from the status quo leader was in the process of challenging conventional wisdom. Effective leaders will challenge thinking. True leaders respect opinions that are backed up by rationale. And then when something requires change, true leaders recognize the risk that some people will not agree.

Here's the thing, you will never make everybody happy. Change is hard for people to accept and resistance is their way of maintaining some level of control. As a leader, you have to have the courage to make a decision based on careful analysis and just as importantly going with your gut. Your gut will never steer you wrong. With that combination of justification and gut, you have the highest probability of making a solid decision that has the potential to garner the results you are seeking.

Leaders Are Mindful

The greatest gift I ever received was being laid off of my job in 2008, with the major downturn of the economy. At the time, I was at a consulting firm, earning an excellent salary and working on client projects that I thought were fulfilling at the time. Upon hearing of my impending doom and receiving the pink slip, I remember very well the pathetic feeling I felt. I had packed up all my personal belongings in a cardboard box and walked out feeling sick to my stomach because I realized in that moment that all of my hard work, actually meant nothing. I was still laid off.

Being unemployed was depressing for me at the beginning. After a couple of weeks of deep self-pity paired with guacamole and chips, I dusted myself off and realized it was time for me to figure out my next moves. I began reading different books at the library to pass the time when I was not looking for work. One of the books I picked up was *Rich Dad, Poor Dad* by Robert Kiyosaki. In short, Kiyosaki completely blew me away with a revolutionary thought (to me anyway) that working as an employee was not the only way to live. He encouraged people to see their way out of the employee mentality and understand that starting a business was not only more financially lucrative (when done right) but also could be more fulfilling. I was astounded by the prospect of owning my own business but I didn't know where to start. In the meantime, I was hired back in Corporate America, but something changed within me in a big way. I know that with entrepreneurship I could better control my financial outcome. Over an eighteen month period I prepared myself financially for my exit.

Once I left my job, I remember the initial excitement, thinking to myself, "I am such a badass...I am boss-free!" Looking back now, I realized how completely delusional I was. Financially, my husband and I were prepared. What I was not prepared for was the mental fortitude that would be required. For a good three months after I left my job, I felt completely out of body and thought to myself, "Oh my God! What did I do?" I was full of anxiety and self-doubt. I was panicked at the idea that I wasn't going to receive a paycheck every two weeks no matter what. At the time, I was working with a business coach who helped me with the mindset side of the equation especially since I was inconsolable about my decision. He challenged me to get around people who had what I was working towards and who could elevate my thinking. I took his advice and signed up for an entrepreneur event on blind faith, hoping that I would be able to discover the secrets to success.

The event was just what I required for the very simple reason that I met someone who would later become a mentor. He opened my eyes to the idea that I could create my results, I did not have to depend on a salary. I had the ability to create my financial future. Did you get that? *Create* is the operative word there. That is the difference. However, in order to create the abundance I was looking to attract, I had to work on my mindset. I had to empower myself with the right type of thinking. I had to give up the idea that I had to struggle.

That one meeting with my new found mentor changed everything for me. I started reading countless books on mindset by authors such as, Napoleon Hill, Wallace Wattles, Raymond Holliwell, Don Miguel Ruiz, Wayne Dyer, Tony Robbins and countless other authors to whom I owe my thinking.

This is not about just positive thinking; this is about the power of focus and the power of controlling your thoughts. You have to infuse your thinking with not only intention but with specific focus and you must understand how to maintain a sense of control with your emotions.

I have had the good fortune of meeting incredibly successful entrepreneurs. In almost all cases, these ultra-successful people have a strong sense of self and understand how their mindset directly correlates to their results. This is not about just "wishing" what you want to achieve or simply thinking about your goals like what you might have heard in books like *The Secret.* This is about understanding that your inner world creates your outer world. Your results are a reflection of your mindset + The Law of GOYA. What is that you ask? John Assaraf, the author of *The Answer,* coined that acronym which means The Law of "Get off your ass." It is only with action that results happen.

Once you have the right focus and action, you can offset the negativity and the self-doubt that would otherwise creep in. Leaders understand the principles of having a solid mindset and high emotional intelligence. It is this emotional intelligence that allows them to lead where everybody wins, it is not about me, it is about "we." That is how leaders gain respect and appreciation because of their ability to create something worth following. Once you understand that mindset is at the center of the results you can create, you will find a higher degree of fulfillment.

The next time that you are faced with uncertainty which could creep into even more negative emotions such as fear, self-doubt and anxiety, just remember that YOU have the ability to switch thinking that is not serving you. You are the one in control of whatever is playing in your mind all the time. Stand guard at the doorway of your mind, be rock solid about protecting your mindset especially when the naysayers will challenge your thinking. They have a funny way of creeping up and draining your energy, but only if you let them.

Leaders Are Authentic

Emotional intelligence as defined means the capacity to be aware of, control, and express one's emotions. It's also the ability to handle interpersonal relationships judiciously and empathetically. Basically, in my opinion, it means being authentic, showing vulnerability and as a leader you are creating a culture. Culture is the lifeblood of any thriving organization. Be protective of your culture for your team, for your business or your friend's circle. It sets into effect a greater good or can also be the demise of your group if you allow the culture to be compromised.

I have seen people with leadership titles that operate with a whole lot of ego. Ego is dangerous. Ego is self-serving, self-promoting and focused on self-importance. Ego is when someone is 100% focused on themselves and not coming from a place of reciprocity. Leaders that lead with ego will ultimately crash and burn both figuratively and literally. High ego is exhausting not only for the person with the big ego but also the people on the receiving end of their egotistical actions. Have you ever been around someone with high ego? Probably, right? Do you respect them? Probably not. In fact, people with high ego desperately seek the respect that they are actually repelling by their selfish actions. It is a dangerous way to live.

Conversely, leaders who are authentic demonstrate appreciation. They are deliberate in their actions operating from a place of serving. They understand the Law of Reciprocity. To get, you first have to give. Actually, most authentic leaders give without the expectation that they are going to get from that specific person. It's as though they set the act of giving out into the ethers, knowing that it will come back to them. They don't ask how, they just set the energy of giving in motion. It is so rewarding to work and collaborate with these types of leaders. They earn respect and loyalty from their employees, peers and mentors who ultimately also often become their close friends. It is a fulfilling way to operate in the world where that focus translates into abundant flow and rewards beyond measure.

Leaders Are Continuous Learners

In my opinion, one of the greatest feelings is the feeling of accomplishment. I'm fueled by it, whether it's finishing a book, completing a course, finishing a great client engagement or project, I love the feeling of closing a chapter successfully. With each new opportunity, the seed of possibility, exploration and learning is available. One thing I know for sure is that continuous learning is something that I'm extremely dedicated to.

I remember fondly the deep sense of accomplishment upon completing the Capstone project for my graduate degree. Especially because I started the program pregnant with my first son and ended the program pregnant with my second son. Who does that? (That's for a different book on what women do to make things even more challenging). The Capstone Project is the last project in graduate school that exhibits the culmination of all the subjects learned throughout the program. As my classmates and I were waiting to hear our professor's parting thoughts, he said, *"If you think your learning is done because you've finished graduate school, you are sorely mistaken. School is never out for the pro. Continuous learning or "kaizen" as the Japanese call it, is a level of excellence that is continuous."* Since that day, I've been a continuous learner.

Another book that changed my life is *Secrets of the Millionaire Mind* from T. Harv Eker. Aside from the great financial mindset advice that Eker teaches, I most appreciate a simple concept he shares of investing in yourself. I invest 10% of my income every single year in continuous learning. This is why some of the most prolific entrepreneurs invest substantially to be around other top leaders. I've heard time and time again that if you can walk away with just one idea that could make you millions, well then why wouldn't you invest in yourself? Notice that I did not mention "cost," I say "invest" because with that investment there is a return.

Invest in yourself, invest in continuous learning so that you can be better than you were yesterday. Whether it is reading a book, attending a conference, joining a mastermind, make sure to apply what you are learning. It is only then that you can experience the results of those investments. One of the biggest upsides of investing in yourself is that you will surround yourself with people who are also investing in themselves. They are people hungry to be more, to do more and dream bigger. I love being around people who invest in themselves. That will add to your learning as well.

As you read this chapter, please know that I share my story to impress upon you the importance of these philosophies. These are lessons that I have personally learned over time, sometimes it took many times of hearing the same message over and over before I activated the lesson. If I could go back and apply these lessons sooner, I could've saved time, effort and pain (remember I mentioned that at the beginning of this chapter?). Alas, there's no looking back in regret, but simply as wise advice that I'm grateful to impart on you.

What are your lessons? I would love to know. Connect with me at patty@pattydominguez.com, it'd be my honor to hear from you.

Here's to your continued leadership success!

Dedication

For you the reader, thank you so much for reading this book. I hope you walk away with some sage advice that will create positive shifts.

A special dedication to my family: my beloved parents: Oscar & Esmeralda Dominguez, with much sacrifice, they opened the doors to possibiity for my brother and me. For my amazing husband, Fili, your unconditional love, support & loyalty keeps me going. For my sons, C.J. and Brandon, you are the reason I do what I do. My strongest desire is for you to believe in your highest potential, you can do anything you set your mind to - I love you both more than you could even imagine.

Biography

Patty Dominguez is a recovering Corporate Executive with experience working in Fortune 50 Global brands and management consulting having managed over nine figures in spend. In 2012, she left her cushy job to pursue entrepreneurship. Patty now focuses on strategy development for her clients at *Create Buzz*. Patty is also the founder & co-host of the *Boss Free Society podcast*. Patty lives in Chicago with her husband and 2 teenage boys. When she's not working, you'll probably find her doing cliche mom stuff and working hard to figure this whole work/life balance thing out.

CHAPTER FOUR

The Story Of My Life

B ack in November of 2009, I found myself in a very dark emotional place. I hit rock bottom emotionally and basically left my life. I left my job, my home and my husband. I had gotten to the point where I felt old, ugly, and resigned. I could not even look in the mirror. When I looked in the mirror, I did not know the woman looking back at me. I did not like her, and I did not know who she was anymore. I wanted to die. I did not want to feel the hurt anymore. I had just turned 36 years old. At this time I had been separated for three weeks from almost a 10-year marriage. I was on anxiety medication, not sleeping, not eating and crying all the time; it was so out of character for me. I was always the strong one, the one who took care of everyone and always had a lead in our family. Crying was not something I did openly, not even in the toughest times in my life. I was good at suppressing my emotions. In fact, if I got to the point of wanting to cry, I would get extremely pissed off. I had major control issues, insecurities, suffered from angry bitch syndrome and made those closest to me join my misery with my way of being. Clearly I was not born this way, none of us are. Through all of my life experiences and interpretations, I had become an insecure, guarded, inauthentic, jealous, controlling, judgmental, bitchy, sad woman who lived as a victim. I lived as a victim by being a martyr, being resentful, and feeling sorry for myself. I know I sound like I was an awful person butI wasn't. At least not my entire life, and not without "reason." At the same time, I loved the people in my life and always wanted what was best for them. I would do anything I could to make sure they were okay, especially for my siblings and parents. I really allowed my past experiences and circumstances to take over my life.

On November 11, 2009, my life began to change. My outlook about myself began to change. My personal transformational journey began as I embarked on a life-changing self-development training. Here is where I gained clarity as to how I created the life I had, up to that point. In the following paragraphs, I share with you some of my life story. This will give you a better understanding of why I became whom I had become, my lesson,s and how I use them to help others.

As children, we create our ideas about ourselves, relationships and the world.

The Move

I was born and raised in Boyle Heights, California, with my three younger siblings, Leroy, Lourdes, and Tony. My parents, Arthur and Lupe Guerrero immigrated from Mexico, where they were born. We also have three older siblings that have always been in and out of our life from my father's previous marriage. As I reflect back to when I was a child, there is confusion in my timelines. Unfortunately, the people that might have a better idea would be my parents, or my brother Leroy, who have passed away. So I share with you some of these experiences, without a clear timeline, the best that I can remember them. When I was about 5-6 years of age, we moved to Juarez, Mexico. My father had already secured a job in El Paso Texas as a furniture salesman and had rented a home for us in Juarez in the state of Chihuahua. Before our move, we lived in Wilmington, California where my parents both worked and were doing very well. We lived very comfortably. I had my own room with a beautiful queen canopy bed with the matching dresser and toys galore. My parents were very happy and full of life. When we moved to Juarez initially, everything was great. My parents hosted many parties, and we lived very comfortably. At one point things started changing when my father lost his job at the furniture store. He starting doing dollar exchanges at the border. Soon after he and I would go door knocking in El Paso Texas homes selling nick-knacks and installing door eye viewers to make ends meet. Things were still manageable at the time. We still managed to be financially okay despite the circumstances.

A Celebration Gone Wrong

One fateful day, my parents took my dad's friend out to celebrate his birthday and got in a very bad car accident. Apparently, there was a car chase, a man fleeing from the cops hit my parents as they were driving out of the gas station. My mother was ejected from the vehicle on impact. She ended up underneath the car. This was a life-altering event for all of us. My parents did not come home for days, and no one would tell me what was happening. I remember talking with my cousin, asking her if my parents were coming back. I do not remember her response, but I clearly remember that at that moment in my mind I told myself that I was going to take care of my brother and sister. After a few days, my parents finally came home. They were not the same. My dad injured his back, and it got so bad that soon after he could not walk. My mother miraculously walked away with an injured shoulder and arm. Unfortunately, that was something she never fully healed from. My parents could not work. Eventually, we lost our home and ended up in a motel. My father could not walk, and my mother was unemployed. My grandmother would send us money to get by. My mother and I would walk in the snow everywhere to get food or any basic necessities for my family. It was an awful time. Eventually, my father was able to walk, and my grandmother sent us money to return to Boyle Heights, California.

Our Return To California

Upon our arrival to California, we moved into a trailer behind my grandparents' house in Boyle Heights. They had a pull trailer stationed in the backyard. It did not have the proper plumbing. So my father constructed an addition to the back of my grandparents' house that had a shower and a toilet for us to use. Whenever we had to go to the bathroom or to take a shower we had to walk outside no matter what the weather conditions were. I was often sick from going in and out during the cold weather. My parents did not work and depended on government aid. Soon after moving into the trailer, my mother had my brother Tony. Now there was 6 of us in this small pull trailer. During this time my father sought employment but struggled with health issues.

The Legacy Of Music Begins

My father was a musician. He played in different bands and had a "family band" when he was younger. He loved music and every time he had a chance he would play his guitar and sing. So, of course, he would eventually teach the rest of my siblings and me to sing. I was about eight years old when I first sang publicly in a talent contest. This performance created a new possibility for my family and me. From there, my younger brother

Leroy also started singing. We started singing in bars and night clubs in the evenings and during the day on the weekends for donations. Soon after my younger sister Lourdes and little brother Tony joined us. We first went by the name of the Guerrero Family, but people kept calling us the Los Pollitos because we were little. So before you know it we were Los Pollitos until we felt too old for that name. I was responsible for most of the singing contracts and brought in most of the income. So at this point, we lived off the government aid and the money we would make from singing. My parents would keep most of the money to support the household, and they would pay me some of the money. I would then, in turn, buy my younger siblings school supplies and sometimes even clothes. Since I started singing at about the age of eight, I bought myself whatever I needed or wanted. I do not recall ever asking my parents to buy me anything. If anything, I would ask them to take me to the store so that I could buy what I wanted.

A Loss Of Innocence

During this period when we started singing, I started getting sexually abused by a family member. How it started, I do not know, but it was someone I trusted. It happened a few times between the age of eight and nine. I do not remember all the details. I do not remember ever being afraid; he made me feel comfortable about it. It was a secret between the two of us. One day it just stopped. I do not know what happened or why he stopped, but he did, and I never questioned it. This was a secret that I lived with until the age of 17. I was always afraid as to how it would affect the entire family and how everyone would view me. I felt shame, guilt and disgusted. I did not have the courage to say anything to anyone. This is something that I struggled with for a very long time.

So much happened in this time frame. At one point, I realized that my mother was an alcoholic. She smoked cigarettes and drank alcohol all the time and it drove me crazy. She was a very loving woman who always cooked and cleaned. She was never out of control or abusive. She was always nice to everyone. My mother suffered from depression. I did not know that at the time. However, she used to cry often, and it bugged me so much. At a young age, I would scold her and constantly bumped heads with her. I just did not understand her and to be honest, I was too young, too ignorant, and judgmental even to try to understand her. My ideas about my mother and judgment of her affected me as an adult woman.

The Family Band Begins

From the age of 8 to 17, my younger siblings along with my dad and myself sang and played music. Going into my teens around 1987 we started a family band called The Guerrero Family. Eventually, our group name was changed to Grupo Abril. I played the electric bass, my brother Leroy played the drums, my sister Lourdes played the keyboard, my little brother Tony played the tambourine and back up drums, and my dad played the guitar. All of us sang. Those were some great times. Let me just say, that had we not performed, our life would have been pretty sad. We struggled with having utilities on and paying the rent. We moved a few times and had no stability. Sometimes we had to sleep on the floor because we had no room for beds. It was a pretty interesting time. Performing allowed us to experience different things that made our life extraordinary. I was popular in school, had good friends and was having a blast at that time. As time passed, we got bigger performances like opening for Menudo, an internationally famous Latino youth group. We also had backstage access to where every famous artist at the time performed. We were once even in a popular teen magazine, in a picture with New Kids on The Block. Somehow through all of this, I managed to suppress my memory of being abused. My dad started putting together big dance events with famous Mexican bands, and I was responsible for connecting with them and making sure that tickets for the events were being sold. In high school, I started playing the guitar in the school mariachi band and sang. I then started playing mariachi gigs for money all the way up to my late 20's, and off and on since then.

Although we were poor and had a very unstable household, we had a lot of love and joy in our home. My parents were both very loving and through their emotional challenges always found humor, music, and family as their source of joy. My father struggled with health issues since he was a child. At one point, in 1989, he got so sick, we almost lost him. I always felt like the parent of my parents and my siblings, and this carried over into most of my adult life.

The Abuser And Me

At the age of 17, a disagreement with the man that sexually abused me triggered the memory of the sexual abuse. It led to a shouting match in front of family members that were visiting from Mexico, my grandmother, and my mother. I now remembered, and I threatened him that I was going to tell my family what he had done. Even though I was yelling at him, I could not bring myself to say what I wanted to say. He even went as far as yelling at me "tell them, tell them!" I kept threatening that I would, but my fear and shame kept me from speaking up. My mom stopped me, pulled me aside and asked me what was going on. I was not the kind of person that was disrespectful to anyone; this was so out of character for me. I told her what happened. She was so angry. She told me not to say anything anymore and that he would pay for it. She said that we were going to make sure he lost everything. Right after this conversation my mom went to join him, as he was her drinking partner and carried on as if nothing happened. My mother and I did not speak of this again until a few weeks later, where she shared with me that she told my father what had happened. She said that my father had confronted my abuser, and they got into a loud argument. I do not know what was the outcome of the argument. My father and I never spoke of this until my 30's. Eventually, a few family members were made aware of my accusations, but no one really had a real conversation with me about this ever again. I was afraid of what it would do to the family if I pursued legal charges, so I internalized it and dealt with this on my own. For years it bothered me that no one ever asked me how I was doing or if I was getting any kind of help. I felt very alone in my experience. It was such a challenge for me because I had so much anger and resentment towards this abuser and yet I had to see him all the time at family gatherings. I felt that by going to the gatherings, it made it seem as if it was okay what he had done or as if everyone was going to think I was lying. Although I always looked forward to our family gatherings, I would always experience anxiety as the gathering date came closer. Many times I considered not going to the gatherings but then I would be the one missing out on my family. I felt like I was the one that was hurt, yet I was the one being punished. This child abuser was enjoying his life like nothing ever happened, and I was choosing to suffer.

What I Chose To Believe

I chose to believe that I was responsible for my family financially. I always put their needs before mine as I was growing and up to the age of 36. No one forced me to; I chose it, and yet I made it seem like a burden and a big responsibility at times. I thought crying was weakness and saw my mother as powerless. Now I find so much freedom in power and in being openly vulnerable. Because I felt I had no one's support about me being sexually abused, I made up that I did not matter. I chose to believe that men could not be trusted, not even family. I made up that people just use me. I made up that my parents gave up on themselves too soon. I never considered what stories they were carrying with them. Instead, I judged them. I could not trust anyone with my life when the people that I loved the most did not take care of me. I felt I could not be open about how I felt or what I was thinking. I became fearful of something happening to my loved ones. I chose to believe that I was not worthy. Can you imagine what kind of life I created for myself thinking and feeling this way? Let me tell you; it was a lot of chaos and more reasons to feel unworthy.

Why do I share this all with you? What we experience as children creates our world as adults. The interpretations that we choose from our experiences as children creates whom we become. Whom we become has us do things that may or may not serve us. Whom we become and what we do creates our result as adults. We are as powerful as our interpretations. Notice what I chose to interpret. What I chose was negative, and it was not going to move me forward me in a positive way. I invite you to look at what have you been choosing that is keeping you from the life you want?

Taking My Interpretations Into My Adulthood

How I chose to interpret my experiences really affected many of my choices in a negative way. I was guarded and had many walls up. I feared vulnerability and felt powerless. I had this win-lose mentality. Of course, I did not realize it at the time. This lead to various unhealthy relationships with men. The moment I would feel out of control, I would shut down. If I met someone that treated me like a queen, I would sabotage it. I did not think I was worthy of having someone wonderful in my life. On my 18th birthday, I eloped. It was for all the wrong reasons. I finished high school and soon after got married. I was not ready for that kind of commitment, and the truth was that I did not want it with him. I had so much regret for this choice. It ended in divorce a year later. I was so happy to be free. I never felt so controlled and trapped my entire life. I felt mentally abused and at one point it became physical. How the hell I ended up there is crazy. Soon after I found myself in another unhealthy relationship that was a crazy rollercoaster. It was on and off for five years. We loved each other, but we both had a lot of personal issues that created chaos in our relationship. By this time, I had some serious self-worth issues. However, I always worked and took care of myself. I went to college off and on but never finished. Since the age of 15, I had a circle of friends that remain close until this very day. They were with me through all this craziness that I put myself through with my relationships. Having that type of unconditional love and support helped me get through this and the darkest moments in my life that were yet to come.

Getting My Power Back

At about the age of 23, I finally went to see a psychologist. It was the first time I ever was able to share openly my experience of being sexually abused, how I felt and my challenges. She is the one who had me understand that I was giving my power away to this man. I realized that by choosing to suffer I was giving my power away to him, and he was as if nothing happened. It was that whole idea of eating the poison in hopes that the person who hurt you would die. However, the only one that it was killing was me. This was the beginning of my healing process. Many years later I learned about the power of forgiveness. I learned that forgiving him was not for him; it was for me. Choosing to forgive him gave me a sense of peace. I could never hate anyone; it is not in my nature. I learned to see him with compassion and still chose to treat him with respect. I realized that my family was in an uncomfortable place and that they loved us both. It did not mean that they did not care about me. It is just not a comfortable conversation for anyone to have, especially something like this that involves two loved ones. I experienced so much hurt and disappointment with my family, especially with my mom. Sometimes I think that it was the hardest thing to deal with. However, I chose to forgive them all too. I continued to go to our family gatherings. I chose to keep a cordial relationship with him. My time was mostly spent with my other family members anyway. I stopped feeling anxious before the gatherings. When it came down to it, it was all a matter of choice for me. I could have chosen to continue to torture myself or choose to forgive and be free. I chose the latter. I am not going to say it was easy, but ultimately I had a choice. I chose to get my power back.

Tragedy, Loss & Heartache A Series Of Events

On September 5, 1997, I had a phone conversation with my father that forever changed my life. My dad informed me that my brother Leroy had been shot. I was playing with a mariachi at a restaurant at the time. I was in the break room during the conversation close to the restaurant kitchen. I started yelling, jumping and screaming. I was freaking out. The cooks came into the room to see what was going on, and my friends were just staring at me. I asked them to get my boyfriend so that he can get more information for me. It turns out that my brother was a passenger in a car with my dad and some family friends on the freeway when some random sniper shooter shot at the car. He was shot in the head and was killed instantly. The paramedics revived him after various attempts. They took my brother to a hospital in Lake Elsinore, California. Our drive to the hospital was almost 2 hours. It was the longest ride of my life. I was kicking, screaming and crying all the way over there. It was awful, my boyfriend at the time tried to keep me calm. It was a nightmare. We soon arrived. The doctors performed many tests on brain activity while we waited. Our family and friends all started arriving at the hospital. Unfortunately, my brother was declared brain dead. With the presence of our family and friends, we said goodbye as he was removed from life support. My brother was four days from his twenty-second birthday when he died. He left a son and daughter behind, and their brother that he was raising. Because our family was so distraught, I took charge of all the matters concerning my brother's funeral services and making sure my parents were okay. I rarely cried. I felt sick most of the time. I know my body felt the shock, but I felt that I had to keep it together for my family. I cannot describe the depth of the pain and the shock. I just wanted to die. It was too much to bare. However, I never took the time to grieve him. I felt like I had to stay strong for everyone else. His death was in the news in hopes that they would find the killer. Unfortunately, until this day we do not know who shot my brother. Despite the pain and the anger that I felt that someone would do something so evil, I made a conscious choice to make the best of my life in his memory. So I did the best that I could.

In May of 2000, I got married to a Marine. This time for love. However, still with my doubts, fears, and insecurities. I thought that it would only be a matter of time before he would leave me. He was great, and I thought that he was too good for me. Talk about feeling unworthy.

On May 16th, 2002 my mother passed away at the age of 47. On Mother's Day, she had a fall. She thought that she had only hurt her back since it was the only thing that hurt her right after. Three days later she had a severe headache and was taken to the emergency room. The doctors thought that she was intoxicated due to her high levels of alcohol. We knew our mom and knew something else was wrong. She kept holding her head; she could barely stand or speak and even started complaining that she could not see. Unfortunately, the doctors left her on a gurney unattended and alone. Although we were in the waiting room, we were not allowed in. My dad sent us all home, and he spent the night in the waiting room. When they had the early morning shift change at the hospital, my father asked the new person at the window if he could go in to see his wife. She was kind enough to let him in. When he approached my mom, he noticed that she appeared lifeless. She had passed away. No one knew that she died. My father is the one who found her. They tried to revive her, but it was too late. The doctors tried to say that she died due to severe alcoholism, but we knew it was not true. When I got the call, I was home alone because my husband was at his base on duty. I nearly lost my mind. I had my sister and her husband take me to the hospital to see my mom. I went in to see my mother lifeless. I went from crying to feeling enraged. Right away I started asking for copies of her file and started asking questions. A lot happened in the next few days, weeks. I had to push for an autopsy. It turned out that my mother had a brain hemorrhage, she suffered from a subdural hematoma. For legal reasons, I cannot go further into the details. I once again took charge and put aside my pain to take care of things, especially my father who was a mess. My dad had just lost his mother three months before my mom. Our family was a mess.

We all continued to make the best of our life and move forward. Unfortunately, more heartache was to come. At the end of 2002, I finally got pregnant after trying for over a year. Finally, something positive and beautiful had happened in our lives. Unfortunately, it was short-lived. At about 11 weeks I ended up having a miscarriage. It was devastating. My grandmother and my mother had just passed away and now my baby. It was too much to bare alone. My husband was deployed, and my family was trying to keep themselves together. I was fortunate enough to have my great friends; the Limon family stepped in to be there for me and nurture me through this very challenging time. I seriously don't think I would have survived without their unconditional love and support. They took me in as if I was their daughter and sister. I will forever be grateful to them. As challenging as things were at the time, soon after this, I became a Licensed Real Estate agent. It was so challenging for me to study and get my license since I was in such an emotional mess. Then again, the next year I got pregnant again. Once again I had a miscarriage. At this point, I was enraged. I was mad at God, I was mad at my husband, I was mad at the world. Every morning when I woke up, I either wanted to die or kill someone. I ended up taking medication for depression for a few months until I was finally okay to be without them. Unfortunately, after all of this, I created much resentment towards my husband. I already had been a controlling, jealous, overbearing wife and this just made things worst. Nothing he did was ever right or good enough in my eyes. I complained about the pettiest of things. He deployed often and sometimes by choice, not military orders. It got bad. I let myself go physically, would not fix myself up and it was difficult to be around me. No matter how hard he tried, I was never happy. It got to the point where he became tired of it. My way of being brought out the ugliness in him. I pushed and pushed until I proved that I was right, it was only going to be a matter of time before he left me. On October 17th, 2009 my husband and I separated, and soon after got a divorce.

The Power To Choose

Looking back at my life, you might say that I went through a lot. At the time, I was not aware of the power of choice. All along I had the power to choose how I was going to live my life despite these events. I had been choosing to live as a victim. Although I always kept moving forward in my life and never gave up, I still chose to live feeling sorry for myself.

Crying and being vulnerable in my eyes was weak. So instead of allowing myself to experience the pain, I would mask it with anger. Because of the sexual abuse, I experienced I choose to be guarded with men. I had this mentality that I would hurt them before they hurt me. I could not trust men, and they could not trust me. I chose to live in guilt, resentment, and anger. I was insecure, fearful, always feeling not good enough, not attractive enough, had a win/lose mentality that always had to win at all cost, even at the expense of belittling or hurting others. I was controlling, living in considerable emotional pain and I was depressed. Most people around me did not have any idea of how I was living internally. My image was more important than allowing myself to be open and vulnerable. I allowed my stories and my circumstances to become me. I allowed them to take over all that was beautiful and amazing about me. So let me say this to you **"YOU ARE NOT YOUR STORIES," "YOU ARE NOT YOUR CIRCUMSTANCES!"** You have the power to choose how you want to experience your life from moment to moment. What you choose can either lead you to success or sabotage you. I was getting in the way of my own happiness. However, you have a choice. You do not have to choose to give your power away to everything and everyone else.

We have all gone through things, some more than others. Take your stories and circumstances and learn from them. Be grateful for the lessons. I always say that God made me go through just enough experiences so that I can better understand and help others. If you lost a loved one, be grateful to have had them in your life and cherish the memories. Choose to honor them by living your life to its fullest.

Looking back, I could have lost my mom when she was in the car accident, and I would have grown up without a mom. I could have lost my dad when I was a teenager when he got sick, but he lived until July of 2010. I was fortunate that they lived many years after that accident. The miscarriages that I experienced allowed me to understand the love of a mother and the heartache of losing her child. This helped me better understand my parents' loss of my brother. So if you are going to make up a story, make up a story that is going to empower you to lead your life in a powerful positive forwarding way. You can do it. It is a matter of choice.

My Transformational Journey, The Lessons:

Going back to my transformational journey that began on November 11, 2009, I really feel that that is the day that I truly chose to live. I was at a point of either I do something, and it helps me, or I would end my life. I chose to do something, and that forever changed my life. I now own that I am beautiful, perfect, whole and complete. I am in love with myself. I would have never said this seven years ago. The most powerful thing I learned was that I was responsible for my thoughts, actions, feelings, and interpretations. I learned that every event was neutral. I created my ideas about myself, others and the world. What I created had me living as a victim. Now I live in responsibility of my thoughts, actions, and feelings, and it has been freeing. I have the power to choose how I want to experience my life from moment to moment. Living in responsibility has been the most powerful thing that I have learned. When I choose to take responsibility for my circumstances, thoughts, actions and feelings, I no longer give my power away. Being in ownership allows me to stand in my power and make decisions coming from a powerful place versus being a victim. In fact, I already began writing a book on this topic. Everyone gets to understand that there is so much freedom in taking responsibility for his or her life. I learned that we all do things based on what we know at the time and our level of consciousness. Consider that we do not know everyone's stories, so don't judge. Practice empathy and compassion with yourself and others. This has really supported me in forgiving myself and others. Talk about letting go and feeling free. I learned to acknowledge myself. I realized that I was powerful and beautiful. I had felt like a failure, and I realized that I was far from a failure. I managed to accomplish a lot despite all the heartaches and challenges. I realized I was resilient and born to lead. All along I was getting the entrepreneur skills that I needed to get to where I am now. All my stories could be a reference to support people in a positive, powerful way. I shared with you my long crazy story so that you understand that we all have stories. We all have been through things. Our stories and circumstances do not have to become us, nor do they define us. Nowadays, I still make mistakes and do crazy things, but let me just say I enjoy my life. I am a work in progress, as a student of life and a graduate of the school of hard knocks. I do not live in beat up mode or regret. I embrace it all. This does not mean that my memory of my past does no longer impact me. However, I embrace the memories, the sadness, and the tears. Avoiding my feelings has never worked for me, and the truth is that it does not work for anyone. In fact, avoiding what we are experiencing emotionally is what eats us up little-by-little. So, allow yourself to experience your experience. However, make a conscious choice that you do not get to be stuck in it. As I still have my moments of challenges, I stand tall and proud. I am not my stories nor my circumstances. I choose to live in gratitude. I truly believe that through gratitude, all things are possible. If you are ever experiencing a challenging time, focus on what you are grateful for. Being in a state of Gratitude shifts your energy and focus and allows you to flip your internal switch to positive. Choose to enjoy your life and use those experiences to forward yourself and others. If you look for the lesson, you will see how it will support you with your business as well as many others aspects of your life. I now use my stories and experiences to empower others to live beyond their stories and circumstances. This allows me to connect with my clients in a profound way. Being open about my life is what has made me an effective coach. This allows my clients to feel that they too can be open and that there is no judgment coming from me. How can you use the lessons from your stories and circumstances to help others?

Every moment is a new moment. An opportunity to create something new, something extraordinary.

At the end of 2012, I created my own company, "Life's Choice Coaching". I officially became paid a business and life coach while still working full time in property management. For two years before that, I took many self-development trainings. I was mentored by transformational trainers who are bestselling authors and travel the world changing people's lives. I did a lot of hands-on coaching as a volunteer. I lead leadership teams and soon after I coached volunteers to coach other students for self-development trainings. With my background in managing multi-million dollar properties from hiring, accounting, budgets, marketing, supervising, training, leasing, and negotiations I felt it was time to start my own company. I realized I had tons of life experience, business experience, and hands-on coaching experience to take on my own coaching business.

Since then, I have one-on-one clients on setting personal and or professional goals, guiding them, holding them accountable, working through their emotional challenges to empowerment. I also coach couples in working through communication challenges and differences, setting personal and couple goals and enhancing their connection to reignite the spark of love. I create and facilitate workshops for businesses and organizations incorporating business practices with emotional intelligence.

I created and facilitated my women's group coaching called "Women's Revival Group." The purpose of this group is to is to support women in their personal and professional life. Here the women are empowered to embrace their beauty, sexuality, sensuality, intelligence, their stories and all that is and all that isn't. As they work to flip the switch into a positive mindset it allows them to take their personal and professional life to the next level. Using my personal stories and professional background, I include business tips, relationship advice, and different perspectives to gain clarity. One of the beautiful things about this group is the connection that it has created amongst the women. This allows them a safe space for emotional healing. For some, it is letting go years of deep pain of the stories that they hold on to, and for others is overcoming their circumstances. By working through their inner conversations and the emotional challenges, these women alter the course of their life. Some have doubled their businesses, others have found the love they longed for, some got the courage to end an unhealthy relationship, and more importantly, they learned to love and accept themselves. I am very passionate about my groups because I see it as an opportunity to empower women to be truly happy and in love with themselves. With self-love, they can really create an extraordinary life. I actually started this group at home. The meetings were at my apartment. When there is a will there is a way, so don't be attached to the way things look. Focus on your purpose and your vision.

To Truly Lead With Success, You Must Lead With Your Heart; Through Self-Love All Things Are Possible

To lead with success, we must have a great relationship with ourselves. As an entrepreneur, it is important always to keep working on improving yourself. If you have emotional challenges that are getting in your way, deal with them. Hire a coach, mentor and or seek counseling. Don't let your pride or image get in the way of doing this. The main thing is that you do something. You got to invest in your emotional well-being. If you want to accelerate your goals, hire a coach to hold you accountable and help you work through any doubts or emotional challenges. Your relationship with yourself is going to have a huge impact on how you will deal with entrepreneurial challenges. Being emotionally cluttered gets in the way of creativity and the ability to constantly reinvent yourself to create the results you want. Be willing to do whatever it takes. Learn to be comfortable being uncomfortable. The next level rarely ever happens in our comfort zone. The first years of business can be tough, especially in your pocket. So if you need to take odd jobs, work part-time or even full-time while you grow your business do it. Use it as your vehicle to get to where you want. No matter what, don't give up on your vision for your business. It is better to get part-time results in your business than no results at all because you quit or never started. Remember you are not your stories nor your circumstance. No matter what keep moving forward even if it means crawling to your next step. Use powerful affirming statements when you are referring to yourself. For example, "I am a Free, Courageous,

Beautiful Woman". Sometimes it is going to rain so seriously learn to dance in the rain. The rain can be beautiful if you choose to look at it that way; Leaders see opportunities out of obstacles. This will support you in not losing sight of who you are and your vision. Connect with others that do the same kind of business. We all have something to teach each other. Do not look at them as competition; there is an abundance of business, and not all business is meant for you. Be confident in who you are and what you have to offer. Your interpretations will empower you or disempower you. Remember you have a choice of how you want to experience your life moment-to-moment. Be excited about all that is and all that isn't. Last but not least, to lead with success allow yourself to lead with your heart. Let your love for yourself and your vision be your guide to your entrepreneurial success. Through love all things are possible.

In closing, I want to thank my family and friends who have always believed in me, love me and support me unconditionally. You are my angels from heaven on earth. I also want to thank my mentors and trainers for sharing their wisdom and changing my life. I promise you that I will continue to pay it forward. To my mom, dad and brother Leroy, I will continue to lead my life with my heart and honor you by living my life to its fullest. Lastly, I thank you for taking the time to read my story. I love what I do. There is nothing more rewarding to me than making a positive difference in people's lives. I acknowledge you for how far you have come despite your stories and circumstances. Everyone's journey to greatness is different. Remember that you are perfect, whole and complete. You are worthy of having all that your heart desires. Be excited about you, be excited about life! You bring beauty to the world, and you are powerful beyond words. Love all that is you. Be grateful! Remember that you have the power to choose how you want to experience your life from moment-to-moment. Your life, your choice!

Dedication

I dedicate this chapter to my mother, father and brother Leroy up in heaven whom left me the legacy of unconditional love. To my brother Tony, Sister Lourdes and my friends who have always supported me, believed in me and love me unconditionally. To my clients for entrusting me with their life, you are my teachers and inspiration.

Biography

Sandylu Guerrero was born and raised in Boyle Heights California. Sandylu is a graduate of the school of hard-knocks. She is a woman of resilience and strength. Throughout Sandylu's life she experienced many heartbreaking and traumatic experiences. She had allowed these circumstances to dictate how she felt about herself and others in a negative way. At the age of 36 she hit rock bottom. It was so extreme that her thoughts were should I live or should I die. Knowing that her thoughts were so extreme she chose to get help. She ended up taking a self development training that forever changed her life. Here she found inner peace and was ready to take on the world. One of the most powerful things she found was her vision for her life and her life's purpose. For the next two years she spent all the time possible in these self development trainings. She volunteered and supported anyway that she could. She volunteered as a coach, lead leadership teams and eventually coached volunteers to coach trainings. She was coached and mentored by some of the best transformational trainers in the world.

Since then Sandylu is now a Transformational Business and Life Coach. At the end of 2012, Sandylu began her own company called "Life's Choice Coaching". Now she uses her life stories and experiences to forward herself and others. With her background in Real Estate and Property management she incorporates her life experience with her business experience. She started by coaching people one-on-one on their personal, professional and business goals. Soon after she created and started facilitating a women's empowerment group called "Women's Revival Group". This is a six week program where the women set personal and professional goals and get coached by Sandylu.

Sandylu's current venture is to bring emotional intelligence workshops to organizations and businesses. Her purpose is to create healthy supportive environments that are forwarding in creating personal, professional and business growth. She is currently writing a book on responsibility and ownership which she finds to be a key to personal freedom.

Sandylu is very passionate about what she does. She has chosen to use all her life's experiences and training to make a positive difference in the world. She is committed to empowering as many people as she can through transparency, authenticity, her love for life and her love for all mankind.

CHAPTER FIVE

When Pain Births Purpose

"He who began a good work in you will be faithful to complete it"

Philippians 1:6

As I was approached to be a contributing author of this great book, my initial reaction was a feeling of inadequacy. I do not have the education that one might expect from someone who would be passing on knowledge about Success or Leadership at this point in my life. Who would accept, much less respect, my thoughts without that? However, God sure has a sense of humor and my mind quickly played life events before me as if I was watching a movie in my head. It was in that place where I birthed this chapter.

Now, you may ask yourself, "Why this title to her chapter?" Because I believe it is a purpose that drives every strong leader. I am sure we can agree that as human beings we all go through difficulties, and no one is exempt from pain in his or her lifetime. Although we may suffer to a different degree, or experience it at different levels, it is what comes in the midst of that time that changes us. However, most importantly, it is what comes afterward that matters most. That is what determines if we rise or if we fall. Often pain can sink us to a depth we never knew existed. Some people become paralyzed by their pain; they become numb. And you can even see in their eyes that all hope and that fight for life has died within them. Oh, but then there are **others** who refuse to stay in that dark place and determine to resurface stronger and wiser. They allow their pain to be their story, and their story becomes their purpose. Having laid this principle down for you, let me take you on a journey for a bit, if I may. And, let me tell you my story so that you may understand my purpose.

About me: My name is Mia Perez, and I am a divorced, full-time single mother of an eight-year-old daughter. Let's rewind to my childhood so you can understand me a little better. I graduated high school one year early, but I never cared for school. Academics were not a weakness at all. However, my passion was the arts! Like most typical Latino parents, my parents did not see a future in that so, needless to say, with a lack of motivation, I started college but never finished. Being raised in a traditional Hispanic family and also in a Christian home, I was extremely sheltered. I was the oldest of 3, and my younger brothers were twins, eight years younger than me. With my parents working long hours outside the home to make ends meet, the responsibility of raising my brothers fell on me. That caused me to mature at a very young age.

My parents were very strict, so I was limited on what I was exposed to. I still don't know if that was a good or a bad thing for me. However, I do believe that had I been exposed to more, I might not have been so **naive to the truth** of this world. I probably would have learned that not all people have your same heart or intentions. Perhaps that is why I was always so trusting, and that misconception, in the long run, brought me a great deal of heartache and disappointment.

Our family was very close and like most Hispanic families, getting together didn't take special occasions, it is just what you do and do often. My parents were both very hard workers, and although we grew up with many limitations, they did their best to give us everything within their means. When I was 21, my father lost one of his jobs, and that was our main source of income.

The housing market started climbing and in 1999 some family members who had recently moved to El Paso, Texas, convinced many other family members that everyone should move, including my parents... and they did.

I am talking about 20 people or more up and left within a few months! All of a sudden at 21 years of age, I was all alone, deserted, in a town in which I grew up. I still felt abandoned. Having graduated high school early and receiving my license in medical assisting, I worked at Kaiser Hospital while I was on the waiting list for the nursing program. I told my family to go ahead and move before I did and that once everyone was settled in I would follow. But, I already knew that I would never move to Texas. I just couldn't see myself there. ME, a California girl in a desert town? NO WAY! So, I continued to work hard and would fly to see my family every 3-4 weeks for many years.

At first, going to barbecues, clubs, concerts and so forth with my friends was great for a while. Especially because, for the first time, I had no one to tell me what to do! No more rules or being questioned. However, deep down I missed the warmth of family, of belonging, and so in 2006 I married a man whom I thought was my best friend because I did not want to be alone.

Yes, it was for the **wrong reason**, but I did not know that then. At this point, I was now in the Lending Industry, and I made excellent money before being married. So for the record, I did not marry for financial stability (contrary to what his friends might have thought, of course, they did not know how much money I made. I earned a lot).

One thing I have learned about myself is that my personality is that of a "Builder". I believe in family, in working hard and building something together for each other and your children. I believe in the value of having your partner's back and being each other's #1 cheerleader. That is what I thought marriage was about because that is what I saw modeled at home. He recognized that and jumped on the opportunity, Me. Why do I say that? Because of all the dreams this little girl always had, of what being a wife and mommy one day would be like, it slowly transformed into my worst nightmare.

Not having finished college never limited me, but it did cost me a lot, and you will soon find out why. Having worked since I was 12 and being very mature and responsible were strengths that followed me in every job. He, on the other hand, had his bachelor's in Business and Marketing and made sure to remind me constantly that I was with "an educated man and one highly respected in the community." We grew multiple businesses together, yet it seemed like they were "His" businesses even though I had my own licenses and my successes were in my own right. At one point I had my own Insurance Agency through Farmer's Insurance, had a wholesale meat distributorship, we had a Real Estate office of about 30 agents, and I helped manage a family-owned business with my parents which was a cleaning company that catered to high-end homes in our community. I was an excellent business woman with many skillsets. Few people could match my work ethic especially when I am **passionate** about what I am working on. In this case, my purpose was to establish a secure financial foundation for my family and to build something for them.

Still, not having an education/degree like him, was something that he always used to lessen me and put me down during the marriage. Eventually, that allowed him to have power over me. However, it did not happen overnight. It never does. Abuse happens gradually, subtly. It is like the frog in that pot of water over the stove. You throw a frog in boiling water, and the frog jumps right out. But, if you put the frog in a pot on the stove with cool water and slowly heat the water, the frog will never jump out because the gradual and subtle increase of the temperature will just acclimate him. The frog will **slowly boil to death** in that water.

That is what it is like to be with an abuser. They slowly and gradually take away every piece of who you are. Daily, they pick you apart, stripping you down layer-by-layer and you do not even see it coming. They cut you, and then they stitch, they wound and nurse you. They wound your soul with hurtful words, and then they apologize, because if they did not "LOVE" you so much they would not get so angry and say those things. Every day you walk on eggshells to make sure you do not say the wrong thing, or you are in a daze still recovering from the last arguments of what "you" caused and you are living in constant state of apology. You cannot even address anything or begin to sort through things in your head because you are in a foggy state of confusion.

And, now you arrived where they want you because that is how they intend to keep you. They take over your life, little-by-little until you have no opinion, no voice... you feel irrelevant, and your sole purpose in now to serve them. They will feed you the scraps of their love and torture you mentally, emotionally handicapping you until you are at their mercy. You are too scared to leave, and you convince yourself that it is better to stay.. so you do. **They target us, the givers**.

He was so sweet in the beginning, though, and I honestly thought I was one lucky girl. I could not tell you exactly when he changed. You never can really pinpoint that with an abuser because they are masters of the art of lies and manipulation! The next thing you know, my money was his money, and his money was still his money. Everything I had was because of him, and he told me that so often that I actually believed it.

Decisions were made, and I was just to go along with what he decided because I was too stupid; and remember, he was the educated one and not me. If I even questioned him, then I was not the woman I claimed I was. I did not "have his back" and I was not "down" for my man the way a married woman should.

The question most often asked is "But did he hit you?" As if, well, at least you didn't suffer physically. What people do not realize is that the worst abuse of all is that <u>which no one sees</u>. Where there is no visual evidence, no bruises or bleeding. What is left bruised, cut and bleeding is the heart and mind! And, unfortunately, no one is there to soothe or comfort those wounds. You are left to nurse your wounds in the dark and in silence. A bruise or a cut will heal in a few days. The human psyche not so easily. Words are embedded in your subconscious, and you believe it.. you become it. Their words and opinions of you will visit you in your sleep and haunt you even during the waking hours. You can't escape it. It may take years to heal and sometimes it never does. While I was pregnant, he would be out late supposedly "networking" while I was left with cold dinners and sleepless nights. I now realized I not only would I always be alone but that I had married an alcoholic. That was hard to deal with in and of itself because I did not believe in divorce and all I wanted was a family. *All I wanted was to love and be loved in return.*

I tried to excuse the behavior perhaps to make myself believe that deep down inside he did indeed love me and that he would never mean to hurt me that way, but maybe the failure of his last marriage still affected him or childhood scars. Anything was better than the truth. The offenses, the putting me down, and then the mind games of apologies and promises became a vicious cycle over and over again, followed with guilt trips. He knew exactly how to play me, push my buttons, and then when I would react he would accuse me of being too sensitive, crazy, and not being the Christian woman that he thought he married.

One night in 2007, I remember it like it was yesterday, holding Yasmin Mia in my arms while I breastfed her on my rocking chair, with tears running down my face while singing her lullabies, one night he finally came home. I had already driven for 2 hours with my infant daughter to the nearest bars and called the local hospitals looking for him. In tears, I asked him where he had been till 4:30 a.m. I was past worried now I did not even know how I felt. Drunk and slurring his speech (like usual) he called me a slut, a whore, and a cunt and that I had no right to question him. He said that I was an ungrateful bitch for not looking around and seeing the house "he provided" for me, the car I drove and the luxuries that I enjoyed.

He added that any other woman would die to be in my shoes. I held my baby so tight against my chest and closed her little ears while she cried hearing his yelling. It is still a fresh memory, and I do not think it will ever become a distant one.

Enduring so much abuse in different ways (which I won't go into details here in the interest of time, but I will leave that to your imagination) drove me to the point of shattering even the slightest glimpse of any confidence I once had. I felt worthless and incapable of surviving without him. That is when I most regretted not having pursued an education. I knew that leaving meant losing everything.

Businesses, a comfortable lifestyle we had built together, and he had already warned me I'd never see a dime from him for my daughter or me if I left because he would hide his money well. And, I knew he would.

Four years later, he has kept his promise, and we still haven't seen a dime for the care of his daughter. He also invested his time well with politicians and boasted about how he had them in his back pocket if he ever needed to get out of anything. I witnessed it myself many times and to this day it is ridiculous how he pulls those strings and acts like this community-driven person when it is just the title and perception he wants for people to have of him.

We lived in an upper scale neighborhood and from the outside looking in it looked great. But, I was like a dove in a golden cage. *Deep down inside the dove's deepest desire is its day of freedom to spread its wings and fly.*

I knew I would have to start planning my escape from this marriage somehow because all my businesses were tied to him. So I decided to pursue my passion, an acting career.

I thought, for certain, he could never claim anything in this new industry, and I can then detach. If you know how abusers are, then you know what comes next.

I was wrong. He first acted like he would support it and gave me this speech of how he owed it to me because I had been a good woman and he knew he messed up our marriage, so he was going to support me for my daughter's sake.

At this point, we were no longer together, but since he would not move out, we agreed just to share the same house (or "play house"). He saw I hit the ground running and doors opening for me right away. Next thing you know, if I wanted to go to LA, he had to go with me, and I had to introduce him to all my contacts.

Long story short, he burned me with my connections, and now he was Mr. Latino Hollywood Producer saying he has all these investors in Silicon Valley that needed to park their money and were willing to invest in Hollywood projects. Right away I walked out of that and next thing you know. While he was out at Hollywood parties and red carpets, I was the one at home, except at times, it was with no running water or PG&E shut off, and I had no access to money.

My fridge was empty, and since he wanted to make sure I did not go anywhere, he did not leave me any money either. I would have to drive to my parents' house down the street to drop off Yasmin, and I would lie to my parents that I was running behind just so I could take a shower there. At night, I would make up any excuse to tell my parents it was getting too late at some event for me and that my daughter should sleep there.

In reality, I just couldn't bring my daughter home to a house that wasn't fully functional. Sometimes I had to come home to light candles and turn on flashlights. It is then that I experience some of my lowest points and my severe misery.

People made comments that my daughter, pretty much, lived with my parents or was being raised by them since she was always at their house. My heart would break because I felt like such a bad mother. *You know that feeling when your eyes well up with tears with a knot in your throat, and you have to look away before you fall apart?* That was an all too familiar feeling. It was hard having to stay silent when I was only protecting her from the unpredictability. Not knowing what was in store for me at home, because I never knew what condition he would be in when I arrived.

My faith was tested greatly during these times, and I would ask God how could He allow me to suffer so much if he loved me. I remember hiding under the sheets, crying myself to sleep in the dark … without a husband, without my baby, just my two dogs (Leyla and Fancy). As I saw the last flicker of light from the candle before it burnt off, I recall whispering to the candle, saying "I know just how you feel" … it had given all *it had and so had I.*

The once young successful businesswoman, whom people looked up to that ran multiple businesses and was always in control, now had no control over her own life. Eventually, I did leave, but it took years. One day, he lost a court case where he was sentenced to 6 months of house arrest and during this time he failed drug tests that tested positive for drug use.

He was then sent to the county jail to finish his last month. It was an event that I used to break the silence and show my family that I was not the crazy woman he painted me to be. I had tried to leave once before, but no one believed me which I don't blame them because I stayed quiet for so long. How were they to know what was happening? Besides, he is a great pretender, and perhaps the best con artist you would ever meet. He could manipulate any situation and still leave you thinking that it was your idea. He will tell you that snow is black because he said it was and after a little while of back and forth exchanges you accept that new information with a smile on your face.

I still don't know who was the better actor of the both of us (even though I was the actor by profession). If you saw our Facebook page you would think I have it all together with my projects and accomplishments and always smiling but little would you know of everything hiding behind that smile. If you saw his Facebook, you saw Red Carpets, expensive hotels, traveling, golf, rubbing elbows with celebrities and politicians while always talking about how he loved his children and his never failing to quoteScripture...LOL!... The power, influence, and illusion of social media. You can "pretend" to be anything you want to be!

Back to my story, I finally had the proof that I needed, that what I had been living in was indeed was a nightmare. My parents took immediate action and moved into my home, and that forced him to leave that same day. Thank GOD!

Since I am a music lover, I celebrated my "freedom" by giving myself a gift that I promised myself for a long time if and when the day came that I could get rid of my ex in my life. It was attending a Bachata concert of Hector El Torito. I had to hear him sing the song that every time I listened, I would tell myself "One day I will sing along with him and feel every word when he performs it live." The song is titled "Me Voy De La Casa". And let me tell you, that night was magical and for once in many years, *I finally felt what it was like to be free once again!*

That was in 2013. Fast-forward to today: I am still in and out of court with a three-year restraining order and court-supervised visitation due to his drug and alcohol abuse (which is ridiculous how he still denies even to the judge in court and everyone in the courtroom just shakes their head.) He continues to make our life a living hell, to the point that even though he destroyed every business we ever had, threw away all the money, and left me in financial ruin. He can't even let me keep the home to raise our daughter in, so I am losing my home in foreclosure as I write you this chapter.

Yes, he threatened me that he would never have to lift a finger, because his family would never allow his hands to be tainted and that I would easily disappear if he gave the instructions. Whether he said this because he was under the influence of drugs and alcohol at the time, I don't know. But it was said many times in the same manner and with the same intention.

So, am I putting myself in danger by putting this information out there? Perhaps. But, I refuse to stay quiet now because I know there are many women currently, who have been or might be in this situation in the future. I need them to know they are **Not Alone** and that I understand what they are going through. I want them to know that there is no judgment from me, and I will use my testimony to bring hope and healing to them and other victims of domestic violence.

Now, the question all people ask when they know of a friend or family member has an abusive relationship "Why don't you just leave," or "Why didn't you leave sooner?" All I can tell you is, unless you have been in our shoes, you would never know the paralyzing fear that abusers instill to assure their prisoner does not escape. This man almost destroyed my life, nearly ruined my acting career and I have had to undergo extensive therapy until now for my daughter and myself to simply get a grip on life again.

So why did I just share all this extremely personal information with you? The reason why I share this is that it has now come full circle. Remember where my **feeling of inadequacy** came from? This is where my insecurity of not having credibility or people caring about what I had to say originated. Because I do not have that solid education "he had," and because he drilled that into me so much, it took me time and practice to reprogram my mind to see myself differently. At one point, I was diagnosed with severe C PTSD(Complex Post Traumatic Stress Disorder) coupled with anxiety and depression. I could have easily used that as an excuse to sit this one out and let life pass me by.

"Woe is me!" I went through something so traumatic that scarred me for life. Instead, I decided NOT ME! I will take all of this pain, all of those years of tears, and with God's strength, I will heal first and then go back for the rest of those who suffer. The ones that don't know how to recover, or those who feel it is impossible to do so, I WANT TO GIVE THEM HOPE.

I have had the honor to speak to women who have survived Domestic Violence, and I have addressed teenagers on recognizing the signs of abuse as well. I made the decision to allow my pain to birth my purpose, and I am using my story to help others on this journey of healing.

I want my daughter, one day, to be proud of her mother (although I shelter her from a lot of the information I have opened up to you until she is old and mature enough to cope with this). She will grow up and recall the struggles we faced. She will remember that her mother never threw in the towel. She will remember that I fought tooth and nail for her and for myself to get back up with the help of the Lord who never abandoned us.

Now, it may seem unbelievable but I guarantee you there are more stories like mine out there. I walked away and lost it all, but God in his infinite mercy set me on the path of my passion, and today my parents are my biggest cheerleaders and supporters. It is here that I found my voice through my healing. It is that in-between time, though, that *period of transformation* that molded me into who I am today.

I am considered a leader by some and for many, I am told I am an inspiration. So, I will not give you a formula or steps to becoming successful in leadership because honestly, I do not know them myself. However, I would love to share with you what has proven effective for me in connecting with people because in order to Lead with Success, once you find your purpose, one must have the ability to connect.

Humility. This is the essence of leadership. It is what connects the leader to the follower through their common bond of humanity. The definition of humility comes from the ancient Greeks. The original Greek word tapeinovB literally means "not rising far from the ground." What does this mean to us and why is this my first point? Because as leaders we may become so caught up in our position, our next goal to pursue or just plain busy with life and responsibilities. We run the risk of becoming insensitive to those around us unintentionally, and we may even forget that at one point we were in their shoes. We must remember to look within ourselves and think back to our beginnings, remember the feeling of our most vulnerable moments and those times that we too were in need of something or someone at some point.

Authenticity. To influence anyone, I believe it is essential for people to connect with authenticity. For this, you must be the real you and not a watered-down version of yourself or an imitation of someone else. As much as you may respect and admire someone else, it is you that people want. Authenticity required me to realize that what I have no one else possesses now nor will they ever. That it is my experiences, my hardships, my struggles, and my victories that molded me into who I am today. Accepting and embracing my past was a process in itself. I had to learn to be ok exposing the raw and imperfect me to help others be heard and that through me they may have a voice and heal.

Transparency. We live in a world where people need to be able to relate before trusting. Trust is everything! People yearn for a connection with someone who has experienced similar hardships and who is willing to share how they overcame them. That was difficult for me to do because I feared, at one point, that in my being transparent, others would lose respect for me, and I would taint the "she has it all together" image people seemed to perceive me having. This is a big mistake and totally the opposite! Transparency opens a door for you into people's lives, and now your words will resonate with them.

Vulnerability. Let's face it, this takes courage! I had to be willing to go into the deepest, most painful memories and show my scars. The fear of being judged sets in, and who wants to relive unpleasant memories anyway? Who would want others to know their weaknesses, or how bad things are today, or have been? But, when it is not about you, instead it is about helping someone else, and you are holding that key, not being vulnerable is no longer an option. You understand that you will save people from falling themselves or giving other hope. I also learned there's beauty in being vulnerable. It is actually refreshing to see this because most people live their lives being guarded, which I get it, "protection." However, if you want to influence others on a deep level, you must be willing to be vulnerable. When you do this, you have just connected at a level most people cannot.

Embrace your struggles. Who does not have them? Most people are more comfortable sharing and celebrating their successes. The great relationship they have, the new promotion, how being your own boss is the best decision they ever made, how their family makes them so happy. Few will also tell you, though, what they have endured getting there. *Every victory has its struggles, and there are many failures getting there.* People want to feel understood and by sharing your mistakes, your struggles and letting them know that you feel their pain helps them know you have been there. Give them hope through that struggle and be their beacon of light.

Never be ashamed of your story. If there is one thing that I can tell you is that the world is in need of more leaders. I wish that in my darkest times, I had someone to draw strength from. Someone I could have looked to and knew "She made it through this, I can too!" I did not have that person or maybe I did not know any better at the time. It is because of that, I decided to open myself up to the risk of judgment and criticism from others. Because at the end of the day, if I can save one life, give one-person hope, or help one family member understand why a person does not leave their abuser, I have done my job. Your story is different, but it is still YOUR story, and you have lessons, pains, and memories that people can draw from. You must realize that because of you people's lives can be changed; so, <u>don't keep quiet</u>. Tell your story and let us all learn from each other.

Perfect imperfection. Don't wait to for everything to be perfect and for all things to align themselves just right to connect with your purpose. Had I waited to feel that my life was at the right place before taking action to write this chapter, you would not be reading it right now! *Often we delay the fulfilling of our destiny because we discount ourselves before we begin.* Guess what? You do not need to be perfect or have your life in order to be able to fulfill your destiny, to have a purpose or to connect with people. Maybe what people need is the IMPERFECT YOU so that they can relate and not feel alone. I pray you learn and see that there is beauty in pain and imperfection. *I would rather be perfectly imperfect and connect with someone than be perfect and run the risk that others feel I cannot relate to them.*

As I end my chapter, I just want to tell you, from the bottom of my heart, how humbled I am that you took the time to come on this journey with me and read my story. I hope that you walk away with at least one thing from this chapter. If you are that one person that discounts themselves as a leader due to lack of education like I was, now you have learned that you shouldn't. If you consider yourself to have too many failures, I believe that makes you even more qualified! If you feel life is not lined up just perfectly yet to start connecting with your purpose, now you know that there is beauty in imperfection. And, I hope that after reading about my life experiences, that you will be more understanding with someone who is currently going through an abusive relationship. Alternatively, you will be more caring with one who has survived one; and that you understand it takes time, healing and someone to be there without any judgments

As for me, I am back in the world of entertainment … Directing/ Producing/ Hosting and Acting. I am currently working on my book where I will go into even more depth about my story and my journey of healing. I have already had the privilege of being an invited speaker on this important topic of Domestic Violence, and I plan to continue doing that. If there is one thing I can take away from all that I have experienced is this, I do not believe God would have allowed so much pain in my life if He did not have a purpose for me. I have allowed my pain to birth my purpose, and I have vowed to Him that I am open to being used to speak my message of hope and be a voice for the voiceless. The way I look at it is this…*With all the "CRAP" life has thrown at me, I have decided treat is as compost to feed my soil (soul) and use is to grow the most beautiful flowers and decorate my garden (life) with it.*

I encourage you to do the same my friends in your own way through your own story. Let us be the type of leaders where we allow our struggles and hurts speak our truth and bring enlightenment to others. Be a leader people can relate to, look up to and find hope in.

✺

Dedication

Thank you Lord for giving me this privilege of sharing what you have brought me through and may many lives be touched through the words in this book. Thank you to my parents Oscar and Esperanza Mejorado for being my pillars of strength and thank you to my daughter Yasmin Mia for being my sunshine even when it rains, my star in my sky and my rainbow after my storm. It is you my heart beats for and through you I learn how to become a better person every day.

Biography

Mia Perez is an actress, a producer, a TV host, a community leader, and a full time single mother. Based out of San Francisco, she was named one of the 40 under 40 Latinos to look out for in the Silicon Valley Latino Magazine. Focused and determined in everything that she does, Mia is thought of as a role model in her community. She contributes her time and resources to charity, making moves for and in furtherance of the public good. Despite plenty of roadblocks, nothing has gotten in Mia's way as she has sought out her destiny in life. She is a lover of the arts and entertainment industry and a woman who never slows down except to decide just what she is going to do next. Seeking to inspire others to pursue their dreams, Mia follows her passions as a matter of principle.

CHAPTER SIX

Beautifully Blessed

"Coming together is a beginning; keeping together
is progress; working together is success."

— Henry Ford

I am both humbled and honored to have the opportunity to share a chapter of my life with you. I pray that it is received with all the love and encouragement it was intended to bring, and leads you down the right path to success.

"Deep in their roots, all flowers keep the light."

— Theodore Roethke

An inner light drives those who reach the point of success. We are individuals shaped not only by our thoughts and actions but also by our experiences, our memories, and our families. It is our power to be aware of our thoughts, invest in ourselves and continue to be the best version of ourselves by learning from those around us. We all have our own unique story, and this is mine.

As women, we tend to be natural givers and caretakers. We take care of our families, our spouse/significant others, our children, parents, siblings, etc., but what we need to remember is we can only provide for those around us if we first take care of ourselves. If we do not focus on our health – physically, mentally, emotionally and financially – we will never have the ability or strength to help anyone else. This is challenging, especially for Latinas, because we have such strong family values.

I am the first of my family to be born in the United States.

My mother, the root of my beginning, provided me with the most selfless gift a mother could give her child. I will forever be eternally grateful that she had the courage and strength to move to this country as a young single woman, to give me a better life full of endless opportunities.

My mother had the perfect role model. My Costa Rican grandmother, Nana, is the most admirable person I know and has been my constant love and support as well as my personal energetic cheerleader and life coach. Her relentless drive and compassion have been what drives me to be just like her. She always pushes me forward to learn, to forgive, and to love, no matter the age or circumstances. Nana is wise; she is my foundation. Her strong family values have served as the strength within our family and keeps us united.

Although I am a proud American, my roots run deep, and my heart still beats with my Costa Rican heritage. I have Nana to thank for that. During my infancy, she spoke to me consistently in Spanish giving me the teachings of humility and strength. I was blessed to live in a multi-cultural and bilingual home with strong Christian values. And, I am truly grateful for this gift because it has given me an opportunity to learn from my family, understand them, and live through the light of God. Might I add knowing Spanish and English has opened many doors in my career today? ¡Soy Tica de Corazon, pura vida!

> **"Family isn't defined only by last names or by blood;**
> **it's defined by commitment and love."**
>
> – Dave Willis

I have lived a life of abundance of love from my family. Imagine the "modern family" in the eighties. We were not wealthy, but we had each other. Two other influencial people in my life have been my godparents, Papa and Lucy. Papa is from Holland, and Lucy is from Costa Rica. Although not my biological father, Papa is my "father" and a key contributor to a source of unconditional love. As for Lucy, she was my mother who made delicious meals and kept our home in order. She showed me her love through her actions. We took family trips; we explored different hiking trails, and we celebrated holidays and birthdays together. These were some of the happiest days of my life. I felt safe. I felt loved.

As for Papa, he was always stimulating my brain. He would ask me questions about school and my lessons, and would teach me new words and chemical formulas on the way to school. What I did not realize back then was that Papa's influence would not only have an impact on me as a person, but it would directly affect the course of my career. Papa would always take me with him to Silver Dollar Realty, where he worked, on the way to my elementary school. Thinking back on those days, it gives me shivers that our paths are almost pre-determined.

As a real estate professional for the last 18 years, I realize that those days walking into Silver Dollar Realty were symbolic moments that happened early on in my life. They made the future bright and created the belief of my having an inner purpose … that I was set up for something grand. It is the commitment and love of my dear Papa that has led me to my promising present and future.

As for my biological father, I would have never known that two decades later I would have built an incredible relationship with him and my newfound siblings. The similarities we share are not only physical but also our habits and ways of being are both eye-opening and enlightening. It has brought me such joy learning about my late grandparents and their life in Spain, while also discovering there is a famous author in the family who just so happens to be my grandfather. What a bonus and a blessing! I cannot begin to describe how profound, deep and pure my love is for my newly found family.

Forgiveness is a gift we must give to ourselves. Forgive those who are absent in your life, as it could be that they are lost on their own path in life. Holding on to the responsibilities out of your control can cause deadweight and pain between your past and your present. Find the freedom to forgive others and most importantly, forgive yourself. Love is what makes life delicious, so forgive and love lots!

"I can do all things through Christ who strengthens Me."
– Philippians 4:13

Our success and energy are often shaped by the hardships we have in life. When I was nine years old, a stranger entered our family. This person was dark, angry, hurtful, and abusive. All it takes in one person to alter your vision of reality. It felt as if overnight my life was turned upside down; my emotions ran high, and the safety of laying my head down, to rest at night, had disappeared at the young age of 13.

Scared and unsure what the future would hold after those days, I simply prayed to God to remain by my side and since that day He has. I simply found that there were always angels in my life that carried me through the darkest days since those experiences, and I believe that the challenges in our lives give us a choice to be stronger. They give us the opportunity to be better humans, perform acts of nothing but love and kindness, and continue to move forward past the hurt and fear.

While I do not understand why children who are helpless have some unfathomable challenges like the ones I went through, I would not change anything about my life. I would not be the person I am today if I had not endured and grown through the pain I experienced as a young child. Compassion, faith, forgiveness, and believing in myself no matter the circumstances, were lessons I was blessed to learn early in my life.

"I am not the product of my circumstances.
I am the product of my decisions."

– Stephen Covey

The obstacles of life kept growing, and they resembled a beautiful shade of pink. Surprise! Not only is pink my favorite color, but it was also the color of the two lines I saw at the age of sixteen. I will admit that I felt a whole spectrum of emotions. I was terrified, but I was also exhilarated. Scared, shocked, but also excited, it was the color that brought me instant happiness, and I knew my life had just begun.

There was now a bold and fearless fuel in my already roaring fire. To this day, I am still amazed at the instant maternal instinct that came over me. I was blessed with my ability to care and love like the compassion my family had for me. I knew that a human life depended on me and every decision I made from that moment on, not only mattered for myself, but for my son.

I was scared and fearful of my choices and actions as a mother, but a brown-eyed boy depended on me, and my love for him was bigger than my fears. Some challenges and sacrifices had to be made, and I know those were the actions that helped shape and mold me into a successful mother. The responsibility of being a new mother can be overwhelming for anyone, but even scarier when faced to do it alone.

Determined to graduate high school early, I decided to take an early exit exam and immediately started going to college while working part time. I was not going to be another statistic. My circumstances did not define me; they launched me. I succeeded and moved on to the next phase of my life as a single working mother, and I was ready for the responsibility. There was a point where I had three jobs, worked seven days a week, and was both mentally and physically exhausted.

There were days when I wanted to give up and days where I thought that I had failed. I kept going; my Nana's teachings of wisdom that anything is possible through unconditional love built my inner courage. You can do anything as long as you believe you can.

> **"The simplest and most basic meaning of the symbol of the Goddess is the acknowledgment of the legitimacy of female power as a beneficent and independent power."**
>
> – Carol P. Christ

Again, I found myself being blessed abundantly by someone I will call my female mortgage angel. This woman took me under her wing and showed me the ropes of this valuable and lucrative profession of mortgage origination. So much of my success came from mentors and leaders, like her, that God placed in my life to conclude that my difficult paths no longer have to be faced alone. He gave me professional, caring, compassionate, and loving people who saw my desire to succeed through the windows of my eyes, and understood the unquenchable thirst for knowledge in my soul. This was finally the beginning of my career in real estate.

A new door had opened, and there was now a whole new world of possibility, change, and hope. My days were now filled with talks of interest rates, loan-to-value, PMI, ratios, FICO scores, and happy homeowners! I recognized this opportunity as a foundation to build a dream of owning a stable home of my own. It was exhilarating as well as overwhelming. I worked long hours and missed out on many fun things my friends were doing. It took determination and courage, but I had a BIG goal.

When I was 23 years old, I succeeded, I achieved my goal, and I purchased my first home. I will never forget sitting at the escrow office and signing the loan documents. I was signing documents for my new life! Joy and gratitude overwhelmed me! I now had my own safe-haven for my son and myself.

My career as a mortgage originator gave me access to an unlimited amount of financial success, and it was the bridge to my next home purchase. Life was grand again. My son, my Nana and I were in the home of our dreams; work was steady, and we got to share one of Gods greatest gift, and that was the gift to travel and to travel often.

"New beginnings are often disguised as painful endings."

– Lao Tzu

After seven great successful years in the mortgage industry, to say I was unprepared for when the market crashed would be an understatement.

To top it off the market crash, coupled with a back injury and some knee jerking poor decisions, left us in one of the most heartbreaking situations of all. Many other families were going through the same devastation, and no matter how hard I tried I could not help anyone. The rollercoaster of life was in full force again taking us to a new low. Fear paralyzed me. I became mute and unable to ask for help. Devastation and shame took me to a very dark place. When you lose all your material belongings, it forces you to look inward and reevaluate what is most important to you. I am profoundly grateful to have had this experience at my young age as I still have plenty of time and opportunity to rebuild my life while young.

Each experience is an opportunity to grow and learn. We all have a choice. We can sit on the sidelines and watch life pass us by, sit alone paralyzed by fear, or we can take action and be the change necessary for a successful and fruitful life.

> **"The secret of change is to focus all of your energy not on fighting the old, but on building the new."**
>
> Socrates

Determined, focused and ready to re-conquer the world, I transitioned into another leg of the real estate world and began an independent small business of my own.

Around the same time, I took my real estate exam, it was recommended that I take my notary exam. It was a blessing to have my notary license as a backup, and I was now able to establish a bilingual mobile notary loan signing service. Notarize It was born and because of the strong relationships I had developed and maintained in the real estate and lending world, it became a successful and enjoyable business of my own. I knew I had to reinvent myself, and I was fortunate to do so while remaining in the same industry.

"The First Wealth Is Health"

– Ralph Waldo Emerson

Life was moving rapidly, and my energy and enthusiasm were at an all time high. My son was preparing for high school graduation and ready to pursue his dream of serving in the US Army. I then started to plan my "empty nester" dream vacation to Europe, as it was well needed at this point. For years, I had imagined the adventure of traveling the world, and the stars were finally aligning! My dream was about to come true!

I was not going to wait for the right time, the right travel partner, or to be married. The time was now, and I was ready! My first trip was to celebrate my son's success by taking a celebratory trip to Costa Rica. It was during that vacation that I decided I should pause for what I thought would be a quick visit to the doctor, which ended with news I was not prepared for. During my visit, I discovered I had a small tumor or growth which, for months, I had been in denial of and thus, neglected my health. In reality, I was scared to know the outcome. My next trip to Europe had already been paid for and planned; I was now faced with the news that it might not have been safe for me to travel out of the country.

Being the persistent woman I am, I pushed and did not take no for an answer. I got the green light to go to Europe from my doctor. The day before I left for Europe I saw my son off to boot camp. At this moment in life, it seemed like I was constantly faced with many emotions that overcame me. I went from single mom to empty nester within minutes, and now my health was taking a turn, which made everything hard to process all at once. My baby was now an adult and had moved away, and the future was again uncertain.

To overcome the wide range of emotions, I courageously hopped on an airplane and met a friend in Greece. This led to my later travels to Italy and Prague alone. I had the time of my life and enjoyed every single moment!

Most of my adult life, I was responsible for someone else, maintained a steady schedule, and had to prepare and plan for everything. My solo trip to Europe was planned, but for the first time I could wake up at any time I pleased, skip lunch for a gelato, or stay out until sunrise! Discovering new cultures, foods, customs, lifestyles, and meeting new people, distracted me from my newly discovered medical condition. I felt more alive than ever!

I did not know if I would ever be back, I did not know if my medical condition would prevent me from traveling or if I would live past the surgery that was recommended upon my return. That is when I truly realized that health is wealth, and if you do not have your health, how can you continue to enjoy the rest of life's abundant opportunities?

"Tell me who you associate with and I'll tell you who you are."
– My Life with NAHREP

Blue, my other favorite color! Coincidentally it is also the color of the logo of my favorite non-profit organization, NAHREP, the National Association of Hispanic Real Estate Professionals, whose mission is to advance sustainable Hispanic homeownership.

It all started by simply showing up to a national real estate convention, and what happened next significantly changed the course of my life at that time. During this convention, I met some of the most extraordinary people who were speakers, board members, and national leaders who I now can call my friends and leaders. They pushed me and inspired me to do so much more than I ever thought possible. Life was once again grand!

To my surprise, I ended up having my surgery a couple of months after the national conference and things did not go as planned. My health had gotten worse, and there were several complications post surgery. I spent a week in the hospital and waited several days to find out if the growth I had was cancer. I was in excruciating pain; I was scared and was faced with an uncertainty I had never faced before. Life and death were now at the forefront of my mind. My mind then raced with endless questions.

Had I accomplished everything I wanted to do before my departure? Did it matter how much money I had in my bank account or did my successful and meaningful relationships make me a better human?

As God remained by my side, I did not have cancer, but the complications of my surgery had taken over a year to recover from both physically and emotionally. To speed up the process, I realized that my greatest strength from that recovery came from giving and from serving others. That is where my passion and love for NAHREP was created. It was refreshing having such a community to rely on because it got me out of the house and more importantly, out of my head. My intention was to serve in my community and by giving my time and effort; I received the biggest and most valuable gift… I got my life back!

The top leaders in the real estate industry surrounded me; the speakers, the other volunteers, and the leadership inspired me. Their belief in me when I was at my lowest point carried me through and reminded me of who I was. Now I had my why, my purpose, my passion and the unwavering support of my peers. Discovering the joy I found in serving others in obtaining their dream of homeownership has been a gift, and I am elated that I get to do what I love for work!

In just a couple of years, I was blessed with the opportunity to serve as a local chapter president of NAHREP, and I now sit on the National Board of Directors. It is an honor and a privilege to be associated with such a phenomenal group of peers who share the same passion and vision as I do for my community.

"Endurance is one of the most difficult disciplines, but it is to the one who endures that the final victory comes"

– Buddha

Run! Another saving grace after my surgery has been running. After being in a hospital bed for a week, you realize how incredibly blessed we are to be healthy enough to move. So I showed up, amazing myself again, and started running alone. This was a time for me to clear my mind, my thoughts, and to cry, imagine, and plan. Being the social and friendly person I am, I rather quickly met a fantastic running partner who I now consider one of my best friends. We began running together 3-4 times a week, and it was what I looked forward to most in the day. My running angel coached me on the importance of hydration, GU's, and proper running shoes. One day, after one of our long, hilly runs, my running partner asked me if I wanted to join her and her husband at the Los Angeles Marathon. I was fresh on my running high and immediately said YES!

Just a few months after my one-year anniversary of getting out of the hospital, I was able to run my first marathon! Months of dedication and preparation kept me sane and safe from injuries. Again, I found myself surrounded by an incredible group of runners who are now very close friends of mine. In addition to my running group, I found and grew even closer to my Way of Life boot camp family. They supported me before, during and after my surgery. WOL became an extended family, and we were more that a fitness and strength training group, we truly lived a healthy way of life, and I became stronger both mentally and physically along the way. The same commitment, training, persistence and preparation I had for running and strength training are the same disciplines that have helped me attain my success in real estate and life. Have a BIG goal, set your support systems in place, and go! Run! STRONG!

"Why live an ordinary life,
when you can live an extraordinary one."

– Tony Robbins

I was, and I forever will be a woman who is defined by my strength, compassion, courage, humility and my ability to love and forgive. I have shared just a glimpse of my life, my challenges, my changes and my successes, but there have been so many other defining moments in my life that I am grateful for, but have not included in this chapter. My prayer is that through my vulnerability and honest sharing of my life story you will find the faith, hope, courage, and strength to fulfill and live the life of your dreams.

We get to choose; we decide how we navigate through life's challenges and successes. There are endless possibilities when we are clear on where we want to go. Additionally, there may be times when we do not have clarity, and we get blindsided by life events. But, it is important to keep pushing forward. PUSH! It is also equally important to be aware of your originating circle, choose wisely. I will finish my thoughts with this quote from Oprah Winfrey: "It does not matter who you are, where you came from. The ability to triumph begins with you. Always."

With Love and Kindness,
Pamela Valenciano

Dedication

I dedicate this chapter to the love of my life, mi abulelita Nana and my son Omar Anthony; my root and seed that keep me grounded and stretch me to grow. My wish for EVERY human is to know and feel love, peace and that possibilities are endless.

Biography

"Pamela Valenciano is a valued Realtor, National Board Director of NAHREP (National Association of Hispanic Real Estate Professionals), NAHREP coach, a proud mother and a life and travel aficionado. Passionate about public speaking she is committed to empowering and encouraging other women. Born in the United States but from Costa Rican roots, Pamela is fluent in both English and Spanish which has aided in the success of her career over the last 18 years. Pamela is a woman of integrity, strong family and ethical values, and an exceptional light in the eyes of many."

CHAPTER SEVEN

My Naked Soul

It is an honor to be able to share my life's lessons with you here today! Thank you for purchasing our book! I hope my chapter will inspire you and helps you to believe that there is Greatness within YOU!

I hope at least one phrase or story I share here will help others overcome their fears of losing, fear of failing, fear of letting their loved ones down or themselves. Just believe in you and that you were born to be great! Let go of those fears they are all in your mind! It is a daily choice to be positive, to be focused, to be determined, to be righteous, to be of service, to be willing to do what it takes to be successful. Success is not luck, it is hard work! So wake up every day with the will, intention, determination and "ganas" to succeed! You decide no one else! Is the fear of failing worth more than your right to be successful, to be great? NO!! We all have to make that decision more than once in our lifetime. It is a constant daily choice to be fearless, to better every day of your life. Every day is full of lessons learned whether good ones or bad ones, but every lesson is a stepping stone to a better tomorrow!

Why? Because it is from our mistakes and our failures that we learn the most! Embrace every day weather it was a good one or bad one because everyday is a new day! It is part of your human growth towards an education and wisdom that no one can take from you!

Life is a journey of constant lessons, but it is up to YOU how you choose to live your life! Will you Choose a life, of happiness, love, health, generosity, forgiveness, patience, joy, wealth and abundance or a life full of negative thoughts and energy? It is all about YOUR MINDSET and the daily choices we make in life! The will, the "ganas" is within you, it is within your soul! It has always been within you to be great! So make a promise to yourself to always aim high like the eagles that soar high above the rest! You are that Eagle that aims high, very high! Your life is in your hands, nobody else's! You have the ability to be anything you want in life! So let's start with TODAY to be GREAT! Right now, today is the day not tomorrow or later, TODAY!

Today is a beautiful day to say thank you, Lord!

For me, it is another day to love, to be fearless, to be unstoppable, to help others, to be me, to just be great in all I do! Grateful to be a branch manager with Residential Bancorp and to be of service to all the families that trust in my team and I to help them achieve the American Dream of Homeownership. To encourage my team to believe in themselves, to be a friend to someone new, to be a grateful daughter and to be a loving mother to my child. You see it is up to us how we live our lives, how we see life. Life is beautiful don't let it slip through your fingers.

Believe that the glass is always full because you are here today, your lungs are full of air and the sun is shining is down on you with another opportunity to be great! It's a new day!

I love to read but my passion is writing poems or as I say in Spanish "Refleccions" because what I write is straight from my soul, no filters. It is "My Naked Soul" what you are reading today.

I have learned that in life there are no real mistakes, no ups and downs, no struggles, it is all part of living because NO life is perfect. Whether it was a great day or less than, every day is a lesson learned! Those lessons will help you grow into your true great self.

What is that exactly, you might ask?... I am a firm believer that God gave us all special gifts, special talents to nourish and help us be great in life.

I am often asked what my favorite verse in a book is, but no matter how many books I continue to read; my answer will always remain the same...

"So God created mankind in his own image, in the image of God he created them; male and female he created them."

This verse is from my favorite book, "The Bible"

It made me open my eyes and realize that I was born to do great things, to accomplish great things; To Be GREAT because I was created in the image of GOD! We were all created to be great! It is our own mindset, our own thoughts, negative people around you or maybe even those negative words you heard in your past as a child from someone you loved that has tarnished your belief in yourself! Well Stop! Read the above verse once again and believe that you were born to be great! Change your mindset today and watch your life transform into the amazing person God created you to be!

As an immigrant from Los Altos de Jalisco, Mexico, I was a five-year old when my parents decided to move to the USA to save my mom's life. I am very proud of my roots, heritage, hometown, my familia and parents. My parents were not rich or well off but they had strong work eithics, morals and respect for all. My dad was forced to bring us here, to California, because my beautiful mother was continuously ill in Mexico, and the doctors could not give a proper diagnosis. My father decided to move to Southern California, so my mom could have the proper medical treatment and hopefully find a cure. Unfortunately, shortly after arriving in California, we were told my mom had kidney failure and that she would have to have dialysis three times a week.

As a five-year-old, I did not know what that meant. Now as an adult all I remember is my mom always being ill and was often hospitalized! But what I remember the most is her laughter, her strength, her smile, her love for fashion, and her overall desire to live, to be happy, loving and caring. She was grateful to be alive! Her laughter, her joy, her hugs, her kisses and our long night chats are what I miss the most. Oh, how can I forget our big family hugs with my dad (the foundation of our family), my mom the eternal warrior queen, and my forever best-best friend, my childhood accomplice, my beautiful sister Yesenia! Our family was almost perfect if it had not been for my mom's illness.

With tears in my eyes, I am writing this. Because it is now twenty and a half years since my mom passed away. At the very young age of forty-one, from a heart attack. You see her body could not take another day of pain, but her spirit could have lived another hundred or more years. In reality, her spirit still lives within my sister, our kids, myself, and yes even within my dad! He was and still is a true example of what a husband should be. He was always by my mom's side. If she spent fifty days in the hospital, there was never a day we did not see her and spend the day with her. He is the best dad that God could have blessed me with. I have always said that I have already won the lottery with the parents God blessed me with because I never saw my dad yell or disrespect my mom in any way or form.

Our family was full of love, and the only thing that was imperfect was my mom's illness. But, even from her illness, I learned how to be strong and never give up! It was from her that I have learned so much. My mom was my first sales and life coach! She was a representative for "Home Interiors" and she loved it too! She was a great salesperson because she knew and loved her product. She was my biggest motivator... my biggest fan. As a child, I remember wanting to be like "Pretty in Pink Barbie," an executive businesswoman in suits and heels. But, I remember my dad telling me; "Bajate de esas nubes, y pon los pies sobre la tierra," which means Get down from those clouds and plant your feet on the ground. On the other hand, my mom and I would often have deep conversations about her unrealized dream to be a fashion designer. She always encouraged my sister and I to believe in ourselves, to know we are smart and could accomplish all our dreams! Regarding love to told my sister and I to always love and respect the man we marry but never be codependent of a man or anyone else. She also taught us to always stand tall with our heads held up high and to be proud of the young ladies she raised us to be.

Regardless of what my dreams were, my mom would constantly remind me of how smart and beautiful I was, and that she believed in me and my dreams. To this day, I still think of her every day and carry her advice with me wherever I go. It is because of her encouragement that I have always been an overachiever, a leader and the strong independent woman I am today! I just hope she is proud of the women and mom I am today!

In dedication to my mom, and with respect to all, I apologize that it is in Spanish, I wrote this poem a week after she went to heaven to be with Our Lord Jesus Christ!

"MI AMOR MAS GRANDE"

MAMI, TU MI AMOR MAS GRANDE
NUESTRO AMOR ES INOLVIDABLE
PORQUE EL AMOR DE UNA MADRE
E HIJA ES INCOMPARABLE

MAMI, NUESTRO AMOR
VIVIRA POR UNA ETERNIDAD
UN ADIOS NO PUEDE EXISTIR
PORQUE TU VIVES EN MI
Y PARTE DE MI SE FUE CONTIGO

DIOS ES MUY GRANDE
Y EL SABE PORQUE HIZO
LO QUE HIZO

LO ACCEPTO CON RESIGNACION
PERO NUNCA TE DEJAR
DE EXTRANAR Y NECESITAR

PERO SI LE DOY GRACIAS A DIOS
PORQUE TU YA NO SUFRES
Y NO SIENTES MAS DOLOR

PERO AUN QUE SIGLOS PASEN
SIEMPRE MI CORAZON SENTIRA TRISTEA
HASTA QUE TU Y YO
NOS VOLVAMOS A REUNIR

MI SUENO MAS GRANDE SOLO
SE CONVERTIRA EN REALIDAD
CUANDO TU Y YO NOS
VOLVAMOS A REUNIR
Y PUEDA VOLVER A SENTIR
TUS CARICIAS Y BESOS

MAMI, TU MI AMOR MAS GRANDE
POR SIEMPRE EN MI CORAZON

Thank you for allowing me to share this piece of my inner soul!

Am I successful? I don't think of myself as successful because the moment I do then have limited my continued growth and success.

In the eyes of many, I may seem to be successful. However, the definition of success is different for each and every one of us. To many, success is the accomplishment of one thing or several goals and dreams. But success has NO limitations! We as individuals do because we create or manifest those limitation. So, please stop limiting your own growth and success!

My life may seem to be what others would consider successful but I am still working hard and growing daily into a better leader, teacher, entrepreneur, writer, mother, woman, and human being! So don't set limits for yourself, just continue to grow, learn and work hard daily to be a greater person every day!

I hear young adults say, "I did not have a great education, my parents did not believe in me" etc., etc. Excuses, right? Stop! Go and grab a book and educate yourself, listen to motivation videos by great leaders as Tony Robbins, Zig Ziglar, Grant Cardone, Nely Galan and our very own Marcos Orozco. Plus, two great Spanish speakers are Facundo Cabral and Alex Dey. Knowledge is free to all; it is at your fingertips! On the other hand, experience only comes with time. Who do you want to be for you and those you love? What kind of legacy do you want to leave after your last breath?

May your legacy be the thousands of steps you took, and may your footprints be filled with love, compassion, accomlishments and wisdom! We only get one chance at life and indeed life is short because time stops for no one! Wake up, you were created in the image of God, you were created to do great things! YOU ARE GREAT because YOU are a child of GOD!

We all go through different cycles in life! Some easier to live through than others, but they are part of life. It is what we do with those life's lessons that matter. Be Strong, Be Fearless, Be You and those cycles, stages of life will only make you not break you!

I will share one of hardest tribulations of my life. Eleven years ago I was the happiest woman on earth. Happily married, in love and pregnant with my first baby! Living in a beautiful home close to the beach with a live-in housekeeper and nanny. I could not ask the universe for anything more. My life was complete, and I felt as if it would be forever.

But after three years of marriage, my life was flipped upside down; my marriage ended in divorce! And to add to it, it was during the mortgage meltdown. Without a job it added a financial burden to my life. One of my friends told me, "you have been knocked down to the ground, there is nowhere to go from there but up!"

And, I believed her.

But, just eighteen months later I felt I was buried six feet under, at least that how I felt. And I did not know how to get out of that hole.

The man I thought I would love forever, my Ex and the father of our child took me to family court and with cruel lies and unfounded statements, took our child away from me; from the only parent that had cared for her and that she had lived with. His accusations were 100% false! Why a judge would believed his statements without documented proof, is beyond me. Every time I remember the day I had to take our child for the first time to the police station to live with her dad temporarily. I can still hear my little angel's outcry of being pulled from her mommy's arms, it is a sound that I will never forget.

She did not understand why she had to go live at a home that she never knew, with strangers she had never meet before, other than her dad. For about two months my baby and I were only allowed to see each other three times a week for two hours each time with supervised visitation.

I was ordered to go through a physiological evaluation, which concluded that I was mentally fine. This moment in my life (those two months) is why I felt buried six-feet under. When your child is taken from your care for no reason, it is like having your heart-ripped-out from inside. I knew I had to stay strong for my baby, or I would become that woman my ex-husband wanted me to become … crazy. I have never been on any depression medication or anything realted to it, but he could not accuse me of anything else but of this. His lies and accusations at the end brought more harm to our own child. Why a father or mother would use their own child to hurt the other parent is beyond me! But I did not let his actions get to me, I had to be stronger than ever and fearless of his actions! I trusted in God that the truth would prevaile.

It is how you take those hard blows in life that help build your strength. I was six-feet under and could not breathe! But once again, my dear friend told me; "If anyone can climb or dig herself out of that hole, it is YOU! So pull yourself up, dust yourself off, and show them how strong you really are!"

My friend was my wake up call. I had the choice of having a strong mindset to live every day as the strong and courageous mother and woman I am or not. I stayed true to myself and fought to keep a positive mindset. I did not let the negative circumstances or cruelty of others break me down.

Yes, I pulled myself out of that hole that I was in; I dusted myself off, started crawling, then baby steps, then walking. As I was walking my vision became clearer; my mindset became stronger, and I reminded myself that my baby needed me and I had to remain strong for her. I started loving me more every day! I reminded myself to forgive myself as well not just my Ex and who ever advised him to do this unthinkable action filled with lies. By forgiving him and this other person helped me be free and to to be great once again! They tried to break me but they only made me stronger! It's been six years since this incident and my Ex does not follow the court orders to see her and be a dad to our daughter. He is an absent father to our child. There is no court order that can force a father to be a dad or a mother to be a mom. Its either in your heart to be a great parent or not. If you are a parent and you are going through a separation or divorce please do not use the child/children as a tool to harm or hurt the other parent. If you love your child/children then settle it out of court, because no order is needed if you truly want to be there for your kids emotionally and financially. Please do not make your child/children into a Case Number that the judge will only know as that as a case number. As grown adults and as the parents you should not need to have a stranger tell you to support and love your child or children! My daughter carries my mom's name Angelica but we call her Angie. She is my pride and joy, she is a straight A student and in GATE! Her number one passion is reading and painting she has a natual talent for this. She designed her Quinceanera dress at the age of 7. She also enjoys piano classes and dance as well. She is my reason, my rock and my daily motivation to always be great because I am her everything as she tells me everyday! Through it all, especially the ugly custody battle it only made me an even more loving, caring and patient parent. I treasure every moment with her because I know the feeling of having her taken away for no reason what so ever.

You see, we all have choices to make in life. I chose to forgive and let go so that I could climb out of that hole I was in. That is why at the beginning of my chapter I mentioned the daily habit of forgiveness! If you do not know how to forgive, then you will be imprisoned and limited by your own ego. Ego is another word for self-destruction. Live a life of honor, integrity, and strong morals especially if you have children. For children learn from the actions of those they love the most. Choose to do and be great every day! No one can be great and successful for you but you! You have to make a mental and spiritual decision to be great in all you do!

I am on a constant journey of daily rays of success. Always remember, success has no limits, and neither should you. What is that gift God gave you? What is your true passion? Follow those two and not only will you be happy and have a strong mindset but you will be living the life of success you deserve because there is greatness within you!

I leave you with a poem that I wrote on Father's Day for our Lord Jesus Christ.

"TO MY FATHER"

LORD, HEAR MY HEART

GOD, LISTEN TO MY PRAYERS

CHRIST, FEEL MY SOUL

JESUS, TODAY I COME TO YOU
ON BENDED KNEES
ASKING YOU TO FILL ME
WITH YOUR SWEET LOVE

LET YOUR CARING LOVE
BE MY PROTECTION

MAY YOUR HANDS BE
MY GUIDANCE AT
EVERY STEP I TAKE

MY LORD GRANT ME
THE WISDOM TO BE ABLE
TO FULFILL THIS GREAT LIFE
YOU HAVE DESTINED FOR ME

GIVE ME AN ONCE OF YOUR COURAGE
TO OVERCOME ANY DIFFICULTIES
I MAY BE FACED WITH

MAY I BE BLESSED WITH THE
HOLY SPIRIT TO KNOW
RIGHT FROM WRONG
GOOD FROM BAD

JESUS CHRIST, YOU ARE MY GOD AND SAVIOR
I AM ONLY YOUR CHILD
WHO WANTS TO MAKE YOU PROUD
AND LOVES YOU WITH ALL MY HEART

HAPPY FATHER'S DAY!

What is a true leader? For me, it is someone who first and foremost leads by example. Who gives more than is expected and never expects to receive anything in return. Someone who loves to help others find their true potential in life, guides them, educates them, and believes in them more than they believe in themselves at times. At that moment in time, a true leader is someone who has heart and soul, and no ego. Someone who has the heart to care just a little more and a soul to give more of themselves each day to see others succeed. It is sad, but there are others that enjoy seeing people fail and give up. Get away from those type of people; negativity, jealousy, greed, and ego are huge detours in anyone's path to success! Remember we are all great, but it is what we decide to be great in that will determine the outcome of our lives and our success or failure.

Yes, you can be great in negativity too. Get away from this! A true leader has no ego, those with ego will only want to focus on themselves and not others! A person with an ego can never see the greater good! Being humble is hard for some people but not for a true great leader. A true leader embodies strength, honesty, integrity, morals, humility, character, discipline, determination, sacrifice, will, heart, and soul! And, most importantly a true leader embraces failure, the knockdowns of life; for those lessons built character and make the leader even wiser.

You might ask, why I think a true leader would embrace failure?

It is because failure is not the end of anything, not even one's goals or dreams. It is just a lesson learned, a stepping stone to a better tomorrow. Those experiences and lessons of yesterday; whether good or bad you have become wiser with it all. Even the failures in life make you strongrer if you have that positive mindset. A positive mindset equals a stronger and wiser you; an unstoppable force!

Some people can go the other way and become weaker, but that is not you. Your mindset will not allow for any negativity in your life or mind, much less your heart and soul! A true leader will always find another way or path to accomplish their goals or their dreams! There is always a way, when there is will and determination.

¡Si se puede! Yes, you can!

¡Vive tu vida al 100, solo ahi una! Live your life to the max; you only have one life to live!

A true leader must know when to say NO at times. Must know when to just say NO and walk away from a negative or harmful situation. Unfortunately, not even a great leader can help someone who does not want to be helped. You have to want personal growth and success, you have to want it and have an open minded to enrich your current mindset and life. Life is beautiful, but it is how you see it that matters the most! It is all in how you think and feel every morning when you wake up and at night when you go to sleep. Positive energy will give you positive results!

What you feed your mind today is what you will believe in tomorrow! So love yourself, feed your mind, heart, and soul with the love, encouragement, and belief that you deserve the best!

A truly great leader can only help those that allow the blessing of this person in their lives! So that one day you can also be a great leader and pay it forward by enriching someone else's life. You decide the type of life you want to live and the legacy you want to leave behind.

There were so many times I could have just given up on life, on myself but my inner self (My Naked Soul) never let me give up! I have had a few people who have touched my life and helped me during the hard and difficult times in my life. I will never forget who helped me out in life and will always be grateful for each and every blessing. I am grateful for each and every one of you who has crossed paths with me in life! Because from each and every one of you, I have been touched in one way or another. Everyone comes into your life for a "Reason, Season, or Lifetime."

You can always learn something from others even something you do not yet understand or think you need to know in your life now. But, then you have that "Aha Moment" (as one of my all-time favorite mentors says it, Ms. Oprah Winfrey.)

Not everyone that crosses your path in life is there to give you love and encouragement. There will be some that are negative and only want to put you down and crush your dreams. But, you can choose not to be like them, and you can keep them away from your inner circle. Keep negativity of any kind out of your life including people! Negativity is toxic! You've just learned what type of person you don't want to be, a negative one! Someone who is always negative takes so much energy from those around them. Keep them away and never share your dreams or goals with them because they will only kill your dream!

But never lose sight of that cry for help from a negative person. For hopefully you touched them, influenced them, with your positive outlook in life. Both are contagious; that is why those who are around you will influence your life today and tomorrow! Just go out there and infect as many people with your positive energy and you'll begin to see the shift of their mindset to be more like yours; like the true great leader you've become! For every day there is growth and wisdom attained with each day lived. Always use words of encouragement and love throughout your day not just towards others but towards you too.

You decide who is going to be in your life or not including family. Blood family is who God gave to us, but friends and mentors are who we chose in our lives. And then there are those friends that are more like family! If you have a friend like this you are blessed!

Give thanks to God for all the good, embrace it, and let go of all the bad. And don't forget to say please and thank you often!

Take a moment each day to say your prayers, affirmations and meditate. Feed your spirit, mind, and soul every day! For it is all connected mind, body, and soul; they are the most powerful tools in your life! Take care of them, take care of you!

There are just a few moments in time when an opportunity will come knocking so you must be ready, you must have the right mindset to know it and embrace it … because it is yours! Now that you have this great opportunity what are you going to do with it? It is your daily habits that you have been practicing for the past weeks, months, or maybe even years that have prepared you to be ready for that one opportunity of a lifetime!

God gave us free will to decide what we do with our gift of life! Do you want greatness or mediocracy? You decide!! We get one chance with this gift that we call life, don't regret anything later in life. I'd rather say I tried and failed then never tried anything in my life. Remember a failed experience is just that an experience that will make you stronger if you have the proper mindset. With the right mindset the struggles in life will never break you. Never stop believing in you and the gift of life that you were given. The Mayans believe there are two important days in our life; the day that we are born and the day that we find out your purpose here on Earth. Just the fact that you were born is a miracle in itself! You are great so go out there and do greatness in life but not just for you but for others as well! A true leader is always thinking of how to help others grow into their true potential and help them reach their goals! Always pay it forward in life!

For those that are a bit more courageous and determined; they create their own opportunity day-after-day, because success is about growth not about a single action in your life. They are not afraid of the hard work, obstacles, and/or sacrifices that have to be made to attain their goals! Criticism and failed days only make us stronger and wiser. Remember each day, whether a successful one or not, is a lesson learned and makes you one day wiser. You and I are unstoppable, because failure is not an option and never will it be because when there is a will, there is a way!

Everyday tell yourself, tell the world, tell the universe, that You are a great fearless leader! Don't be embarrassed to declare it because before anyone can believe it, you must believe it yourself!

Believe that you are not just here to enrich your life but those around you too!

Yes, I am a child of God! I was born to be great because I was created in the image of God!

Be fearless, be unstoppable, be limitless, be willing to be great!

I want to thank Marcos Orozco for the opportunity to be part of this project and journey. If my chapter helps one person to believe in themselves, to never give up even after life knocks you down, to forgive those you loved and betrayed you; then I have paid it forward! I hope our collaboration of our stories as women in today's world has enriched your life for many years to come! I know all the other amazing ladies here have truly shared their heart with you in each one of the chapters we wrote. I hope my memoirs that I have shared in this chapter have touched you in a positive way.

Always be true to yourself and remember you and I were made in the image of God!

inspired, motivated, driven and blessed today and always!

Dedication

I want to dedicate my chapter to my beautiful daughter Angelica Acuña Martinez; you are my reason in life, you are why I am fearless and the biggest blessing God has given me. I hope I continue to make you proud! To whom I admire the most and I am honored to call them dad and mom; Benjamin and Angelica Martinez. Mom I know you are smiling from up above, I miss you so much and wish you were here! You are "The Wind Beneath My Wings." Dad, I hope I've made you proud! Thank you for being a great role model as a human being and as a man! To my siblings, Yesenia (my best-friend and childhood accomplice) and Lissandro I love you both to the moon and back! To my step-mom thank you for being a great friend and for loving my little one so much! To my nephews and nieces; I love you, always believe in you! To my family and true friends, I love you and I treasure the moments we are able to share together, especially the ones filled with laughter! To Marcos Orozco our publisher for giving me this opportunity to share my life with each and every one of you! To God for giving me this wonderful life to live, to love, to forgive, to create, to learn, to fail, to succeed and to share with those I love!

I am humbled and honored to be part of this collaboration with all the amazing ladies on this book "Lead with Success"

Biography

Many people dream of success, many will continue to dream for as long as they live without tasting the victories. But those who are passionate enough will make their dreams come true and when they have a warrior instinct such as Anna, no matter what happens or how many times they fall, so long as they breathe they will always get back up.

Anna has the warrior instinct of a single mother with a naked soul that loves life, never gives up as that would mean giving up the passion of helping others. The smiles in the families she helps day after day and knowing her loved ones are well taken care of is reason enough to keep the heart of this warrior pumping hard.

Anna Martinez has given her heart to everything she has touched. She is very passionate about everything she does in life and selective of those she opens her heart to, as it's her treasure chest.

But Anna is stronger now after a series of life lessons well learned through which she has tasted defeat, failure, injustice and betrayal at some point in her life.

Her passion however has never died down, how could it! Mother to an amazing young girl with a beautiful little smile that reflects her mother's bright mind and soul, Anna has fuel and passion for ever.

Anna is a branch owner of three locations with Residential Bancorp, from where she's able to help hundreds of families succeed by making their own dreams come true; the dream of homeownership! Anna has become successful by always helping others accomplish their dreams, reach their full potential or by mentoring others!

CHAPTER EIGHT

Leadership With Values & Gratitude

"When you open and understand your past, accept your present and define your purpose, you will transform your future."

– Teresa Razo

I was born and raised in Laguna Beach, California, as an only child to a hard-working couple from Jalisco, Mexico. Grew up enjoying a normal and peaceful childhood, until May 4, 1985, when my father died, leaving my mother and me in great sorrow, extreme shock and unprotected. At my young age of 10, my world made an 180-degree turn, and my perfect childhood became a daily fight for survival. The entire world was against me and only me, myself and I fighting to survive.

Since my father's death, I began helping my mother with financials, translations and all aspects of life in order to survive. At the same time that we were struggling to survive, dealing with the pain of losing your loved one, there were many negative people. This is the time I would have given the world for a hug and kind words of encouragement, but toxic people were present. All I could hear was….. "What are you going to do? Where are you going to live, you will not be able to afford the rent? You will never amount to anything? Nobody is going to love you for whom you are!" People taking advantage of our pain and struggle to abuse us financially, physically and mentally. Sadly, all of the negativity came from close family members. Today, I am thankful to those people and understand their issues, and know it was never an issue with me, it was their issues and their unhappiness that did not allow them to be kind to others. I have forgiven them. Forgiving people who have hurt you does not mean you forgot or accept their behavior, nor will you trust them again. It simply means you forgive them and let go so you can move on with your life. It is solely for your interest and your interior peace.

"Do not let the behavior of others destroy your inner peace."

– Dalai Lama

My father was my best friend. His sudden death was devasting and incomprensive. Many years went by questioning why? Why my dad? Today I still don't know why but if I could get a wish, I would simply ask for more time with him. My dad was my world, and I was the world to him. When I was in elementary school, I got into a physical fight with a girl named Lupe; of course, it was self-defense. Indeed, there were consequences, and I was suspended for three days. I was scared to confront my mother, and I knew I had to pay even more consequences at home. Fortunately, my father received the call and picked me up. He sat down to hear the principal's lecture and told the principal he was going to have a serious talk with me. Immediately, I thought it meant double trouble for me! We began driving home in complete silence, suddenly he made a turn towards the beach, and I still didn't even want to ask where we were going. As soon as he could, he stopped the car and started laughing and asked me, "So tell me what happened? I didn't know you would fight? How did you punch her?" So I told him what happened, and he said, "next time make sure you hit her harder so everyone knows they cannot make fun of you." I could not believe what I was hearing... I remember saying, "but dad, if I hit her harder I will get in more problems." He looked at me and said "I will always be there to help you, even when you don't see me! Don't start the fight, but if you have to defend yourself and be smart and hit harder". That day he made it clear that physical fights are only for self-defense and realized that words and actions are more powerful than fists. He promised not to tell my mother about my suspension, there was simply no school due to teacher training. In the meantime, we enjoyed our three days at the beach, mall, and Disneyland. My daddy was that awesome type of friend and daddy!

I clearly remember sitting in a corner of our apartment with my dad's picture and remembering his last words.... "promise me you will never give up, and you will continue your education." That day I decided to never give up, I was going to keep going to matter what people said or thought... it was a promise to my daddy!

After graduating from Laguna Beach High School, I was accepted to several universities and decided to stay home and attend the University of California, Irvine where I graduated in 1998 with a Spanish major and studies in Chicano Latino & Criminology. I decided to stay home for several reasons and due to lack of funds. Attending college was a hardship on my mother who already cleaned 2 to 3 homes 6-days a week so we could survive. I was not going to put more pressure on her, so instead of UC Berkeley I decided UCI. It took me 5 years to graduate since the last couple years I took fewer units so I could work full-time. Many, many times I had a decent breakfast at home and skipped lunch at school in order to save and have enough money for books and parking for the semester. Most of the time a banana was my best friend during lunch. When I was hungry, I opened my journal and started writing.... I made timelines of goals, then described each goal with details, and then concentrated on my reading and homework. Writing about my goals at the beginning enabled me to focus on goals and keep my mind off my growling stomach.

Always eager to learn and unconsciously keeping my promise to my dad, I continued various educational sessions, seminars and events. Obtained my certification as an Accredited Pension Administrator and continued my education with seminars and conventions. In 2015 graduated from the Latina Women's Leadership and Entrepreneur Program from USC for a life changing experience, continued to the Stanford Latino Entrepreneur Leaders Program in 2016. Education has been an important aspect of my life, and I have realized I have been unconsciously continued my education to increase my knowledge, but most important to make sure my daddy would be proud of her little girl who promised to continue her education. With immense gratitude and honor, today, I know my daddy is proud of his little girl.

After 18 years as a senior pension administrator, specializing the Defined Benefit Plans I began to help my husband with his restaurant business. Helping my husband was quickly just an excuse, the business became my passion and the vehicle to empower and help others. Discovering entrepreneurship has been amazing. It goes naturally with my personality and beliefs. Nothing better than working hard, then playing and helping harder.

Life has not been easy, still not easy, but the gratitude inside my heart makes it a perfect world with imperfections. My goal today and commitment to you is to share key elements that took me years to discover. To share and empower anyone to find himself or herself and live life so we can together make a difference to many more people and lift up our communities. I want to inspire people to follow their passion and work hard for their dreams. I want to encourage people to work with passion to conquer their dreams. Although life has not always been colorful, I have been blessed in many aspects of my life. Today I am currently married to an amazing, humble man, Leo and mother of two amazing boys, Luis and Emiliano. They have been my biggest blessing in life and will always be my greatest treasure.

We all face difficulties in life. How we encounter these difficulties is how we learn. Always remember your ATTITUDE DETERMINES YOUR ALTITUDE. Great attitude, takes you to a greater altitude. Negative attitude takes you down and will slowly suffocate you.

The first and toughest task is to be authentically true to yourself. When you are true to YOU, there are no limits! Open and understand your past. Even if it hurts, open it and own it. If necessary seek help, there is nothing wrong with professional help, know you are not alone in this world. Know things happen for a reason and it is okay to not be perfect. It's healthier to be happy, than perfect. Identify, accept and love your good and bad qualities. You are one of a kind, look around, there is no one exactly like you! Be honest with yourself, be you, don't be who you think you should be, nor what others want you to be. Ask yourself what makes YOU happy? What gives YOU peace and satisfaction? When you can be you and be proud of who you are, things change! The universe changes and aligns. One cannot be authentic to others if you cannot be authentic to yourself.

As we can all relate, life is not easy, and we all go through ups and downs, facing obstacles, some small, some larger, but they are still obstacles. These obstacles are only learning experiences. Nobody said life was easy, it is up to you to make a life of gratitude and fulfillment. Again, attitude is your best friend. It is not the problem, it is the way you see and approach the situation that makes the difference at the end. My attitude, "I never lose, I either win, or I learn."

Living Your Present

Many people concentrate on what they don't have and what they want to have. Having goals and ambition to achieve more and more is great, but never forget to be grateful for what you have. No matter how good or bad you think your life is, wake up each day and be thankful for your life. Someone somewhere is fighting to survive.

Today I am grateful for everything I have, especially my health, my family, friends and my business life. My family is my biggest treasure and the most important aspect of my life, they are the engine and fuel to keep me going even in the toughest moments. Sometimes it feels like I am a salmon swimming against the current, but I sure do have the energy and attitude to "just keep swimming."

I am thankful to run the operations of both the restaurant and market at Villa Roma Argentine & Italian in Laguna Hills. Our restaurant and market proudly are run with values. We are not perfect, but we sure are proud to always do our best to satisfy the palate and soul of each of our guests while sharing our food and Latin culture when dining with us. It has been my greatest honor to work with such hard working and strong valued staff. I am grateful and proud of each of our current and past team member that has provided their values, time and love to Villa Roma and our loyal patrons. Today we are honored to be part of an amazing community and blessed to have the opportunity give back in many ways.

Each day we need to be grateful for our health. Our health is precious and should be one of our priorities. Without it, you cannot care for others, and we tend to take care of others first. Especially us women, it is in our nature to care for our loved one and sacrifice our own health. Make sure you schedule time to yourself. If it's walking at the beach, reading a book, enjoying a coffee or simply taking a nap…do it! You deserve it and never feel guilty. It is extremely sad to hear many cases where people invest their life in making money and end spending all their money trying to gain their health back.

Define Your Purpose & Values

Defining your purpose is crucial to achieving success. Defining why you do what you do? The why you love what you do? Really spend time defining your WHY. Once you have determined your why … define your values. Take a few values and make your own definition. Remember you are unique and special. Therefore your definitions don't have to match others' definitions.

Things I have learned to appreciate:

- Love and accept myself with qualities and deficiencies.

- Be a fighter, and never give up.

- I can be a great person and achieve success at the same time.

- It is okay to ask for help.

- I love my strengths and my weaknesses.

My definitions of Important Values:

- Respect: accepting others and myself with deficiencies and qualities. Respecting opinions, culture, beliefs and actions.

- Honesty: being honest with yourself so you can be honest with everyone else.

- Authenticity: always being YOU! Accept and love YOU so you can accept and love others.

- Humble: staying grounded in the worst and best situations. Never forget where you come from. And never forget who has always been there for you.

- Integrity: Doing the right thing, even if others are not looking!

CEO Of Your Life

Have you ever dreamed of being the CEO of a company? Well, congratulations today you start being the CEO of your own life. You can make the decisions and take your life in any direction you want. Since you are the CEO, you can promote, demote or terminate people and situations in your life. Remember you are the CEO of your life!

When I lost my father, no one told me I was my own CEO, today I want you all to know you are the true architect and CEO of your life. Thankfully, I made the correct decision back then and did not give up! Life is not always colorful, it could get black, but you need to decide to put some color in your life and stop being the victim. You have the choice to be the victim and have others treat and see you as the victim or, lift and take ownership and take the necessary steps to change. Remember to never live in the past. The past is only a lesson, not a life sentence.

Life Experiences

It began as a dream to open a restaurant, then the opportunity came. As soon as we shared our dream, we had many opinions from people. "The risk is too high, most of the restaurants fail in the first 2 years, your dreams are too high. You don't have enough money for backup. What if you fail?"

The funniest is that I never asked for their opinion, but they made sure to offer it. Most of the time people speak because they are not ready to take the risk themselves so they share their fears with you. It's like when a woman is pregnancy and almost ready for labor, people most of the time share the horror stories of labor, they seldom share the beautiful stories of labor nor the happiness and love your newborn brings to your life! We took the risk. Was it easy? No, but it sure was worth it. We did and still worked hard. It is long hours, holidays and weekends, but it is so worth it! It is our passion and gives us complete satisfaction.

Then you have those moments where you encounter negativity at its finest. One time I had a person tell me, "you will not be able to succeed in the entrepreneur business, you are a woman, and you are Latina, and you are short and brown skin." Guess what I did? I gave them a chair and walked away. When someone tells you, you are not capable of achieving your dreams, you give them a chair and walk away. You walk away because that person does not deserve you in their life. The chair? So you can invite them to sit and watch you achieve!

What motivates me is the satisfaction to help people develop and believe in themselves. I truly enjoy transparency, hard working people with a giving heart. I enjoy helping people and making them feel they can do better... treating them with respect. I get more satisfaction from helping others, than asking for help. My goal, to live in gratitude and have people say, "because of you I did not give up."

Humble Advice

If I can give you some humble advice, I would say "if you really want it, dream it, work hard to achieve it, and never, ever give up." It is not going to be easy, its hard work, sometimes you will doubt if it is worth it, just make sure it is what you want, then don't give up!!

Be Grateful: Acknowledge daily gratitude; take the time to inhale and exhale gratitude!

Value: Give value to people, before you add value to them. And never undervalue yourself.

Educate: Never stop learning. Take the course, take the seminar, do the network, do the homework and most important take the risk and learn from mistakes. Most important educate others anytime you can.

Travel: Take those exploring vacations. Not only travel the world, but explore the culture and try different foods and activities that will make you live unforgettable experiences. Pamper yourself!

Love: Love yourself so you can love others. Enjoy your family and every moment in life... tomorrow might not exist.

Another piece of advice I want to share with you is to be aware people are always talking and listening. By this, I don't mean words, I mean actions, attitude, and achievements. People's actions and attitude speak for themselves and others watch. I once thank a special person for sharing one of my proud moments on his Facebook and his answer was so astonishingly beautiful, it meant the world to me. You never know who is watching you and more important who you are inspiring. I want my success and mistakes to inspire someone, somewhere and say if Teresa was able to do it, then I can also. Thank you to those who inspire me to be better each day. Forever grateful to make a difference in someone's life. Today, I want to share a beautiful answer to me that has given me more energy to empower my community:

"Tere, I can only say that I personally am very proud of what you both have accomplished. Your energy and drive to be successful is not only invigorating but also very contagious and is an absolute source of personal motivation for me, So let me be the one to thank you for that great gift." ….... Thank you, Edson.

Quotes For Some Thought

"If you are more fortunate than others,
it is better to build a longer table than a taller fence.

— Anonymous

"They laugh at me because I'm different;
I laugh at them because they're all the same."

— Kurt Cobain

The difference between who you are and
what you want to be is what you do

— Bill Phillips

"El fracaso es parte de la vida; si no fracasas,
no aprendes y si no aprendes, no cambias."

— Paulo Coelho

What Matters At The End

Never forget you are the CEO of your life. You are not perfect, and that is okay. People might not like you or what you do, but it is your passion and it is YOU. If you are authentic and live with your values well-defined, you will achieve. It is okay for people not to like you, the most important is that they respect you.

In the end, the most important is your authentic happiness. Don't ever be afraid of change. Always remember, God will never take anything away from you without the intention of replacing it with something much better.

As an entrepreneur, I believe "your smile is your logo, your personality is your business card, how you leave others feeling after having an experience with you becomes your trademark."

– Anonymous

Breathe Gratitude, Love and be happy!
Be Authentic, Acknowledge & Take Action!!

Today

Today I am grateful for all the ups and downs of my life. It has been for the failures and hardships that have only made me stronger. My husband always, tells me "what does not kill you, should only make you stronger." Take whatever life throws at you to build something great and powerful.

It has been an amazing journey as a Latina entrepreneur. I enjoy every moment as an entrepreneur. The difficult moments are amazing and necessary because they make you better and more knowledgeable. Situations arise daily where you have to adapt, change and make quick decisions…. that motivates me. It is like solving a puzzle. We as Latino/a already have an entrepreneur soul. We are hard working, dedicated, risk takers and have an authentic work ethic. Have the passion, work for it!!

Owning a restaurant involves much of your time and dedication, but the satisfaction of doing what you enjoy and the ability to help your community is the best feeling. As a wife, mother, daughter, businesswoman and community leader I balance my life to enjoy my passion, business, family and life. I also embrace the headaches, sacrifices and risks. I encourage you to take the risk…. dream big, but only dream big, but work and act big!

Many times I asked myself, "Is this really worth the time away from my family?" Today, I have the answer…Yes, it was worth it! It is a matter of balance. I have learned to balance my life to enjoy my passion, business, family and life. Today I am blessed to be at this stage in my life. Enjoying my three biggest treasures, my husband, and my children, while running a business and inspiring and helping others fulfill their dreams.

Many people said, thought and believed I would amount to nothing. I never gave up and today I am honored to inspire and set an example to my children. I believe the sky is not the limit; there is no limit... dreams come true, just believe, work hard and never ever give up. If you ever feel you cannot make it.... remember you are strong, and somewhere there is another person who made it so why not you!! If in doubt, reach out to me and always remember to never, ever give up!

Blessings and keep going forward!!

Dedication

I dedicate this chapter to my by best friend, mentor and amazing husband Leo and to my two blessings Luis and Emiliano. I also want to acknowledge my parents for working so hard to give me a better life. A special dedication to my beloved daddy!

To everyone who believed and inspired me and still do. To my amazing staff at Villa Roma

Biography

Teresa Razo is a mother of 2 handsome boys, wife of an amazing man, entrepreneur, Latina, community leader, motivational speaker, board member to several organizations and most important a woman and human being like all of us.

Conclusion

We would like to conclude this book with a simple message of hope and responsibility. This book was written by 8 different Latina influencers with different experiences and circumstances. We want you to know that Leadership starts with you. You will make many mistakes along the way but that's part of the experience. So don't let that stop you from stepping into your greatness! Keep your eyes on the prize and never give up!!

About the Publisher

Marcos Orozco, Founder of Book Launch Academy is dedicated to helping Latina and Latino Influencers become Published Authors to Increase their Influence, Leverage their Message and Expand their Brand so that they can maximize their impact and help more people... Feel free to visit us @ www.BookLaunchAcademy.com